WHAT IS A PALESTINIAN STATE WORTH?

WHAT IS A PALESTINIAN STATE
WORTH?

Sari Nusseibeh

HARVARD UNIVERSITY PRESS

Cambridge, Massachusetts, and London, England

2011

Library of Congress Cataloging-in-Publication Data

Nusseibeh, Sari.
  What is a Palestinian state worth? / Sari Nusseibeh.
      p.   cm.
  Includes bibliographical references and index.
  ISBN 978-0-674-04873-7 (alk. paper)
    1. Arab-Israeli conflict—1993—Peace.   2. Arab-Israeli
conflict—Causes.   3. Middle East—Ethnic relations.   I. Title.
  DS119.76.N87 2011
  956.9405′4—dc22   2010040076

For Sarimir
and the others to follow

Contents

Introduction:
Is a State a Siren Song?

Politics for me has always been a means, not an end. I say this because, over time, I have come to realize that for many people it is an end in itself. Beginning with the heated political discussions I heard as a boy growing up in my parents' house in Jerusalem—discussions by acquaintances, relatives, and friends—and continuing through my own participation in political activities and debates as an adult, I have learned that some people enjoy engaging in politics, pure and simple, never mind the objectives in whose name they are supposedly doing it.

I want to distinguish straight away between politics as an intellectual (academic) pursuit and politics as a bread-and-butter job, a street activity, or a daily obsession, for want of better phrases. I understand

and even admire scholars of politics, those who try to untangle the quantum laws of group human behavior: why people act as they do, how they are likely to act in the future. But outside such academic pursuits, if you find that a discussion about a pressing political problem is going around in circles rather than focusing on finding a solution, caught up in a loop created by the very people with whom you are having the discussion, you may justifiably conclude that those people are probably more invested in the discussion itself than in solving the problem. It was in that spirit that a Palestinian colleague of mine, after we had worked together to set up a grassroots movement to encourage Israeli and Palestinian leaders to negotiate, suggested that we not disband our organization, as other tasks would surely come up—tasks that, as he said, would keep us going as players in the *political game.* His interest was clearly in politicking, never mind what the politicking was about. For him it was less important who scored, or what was scored, than that he continued to be a player.

My lack of interest in politicking (politics as a game) probably explains my lack of interest in a separate Palestinian state except as a means toward an end—toward achieving our collective well-being, or transforming a state of oppression into a state of freedom. I think that some people's enthusiasm for a Palestinian state simply reflects their interest in politicking, or in negotiation as a pursuit. I have at times even suspected some of our politicians (both Palestinian and Israeli) of viewing the negotiations they were engaged in that way: as a game, and one to be played as long as possible, rather than as a step toward getting a job done. I do not claim that people are naturally divided into job-doers and game-players, and I have no problem accepting the argument that one only becomes obsessive about playing games after first becoming disillusioned with the real-life effects of one's efforts. What I do wish to emphasize is that in our quest to achieve something of value, we often find ourselves lost, having been enchanted and hence distracted along the way by the sweet-sounding Sirens encountered in our path's endless labyrinths—and that some of those Sirens may be singing about the trappings of a Palestinian state.

In 1974, during my first year as a graduate student at Harvard, Walid Khalidi, a veteran diaspora Palestinian academic and political analyst (and a family friend belonging to one of the most intellectually distinguished Jerusalem families), met with some students to discuss his then-explosive article "Thinking the Unthinkable," in which he argued in favor of the establishment of a "mini–Palestinian state" in return for Palestinian recognition of Israel—what later came to be known as the two-state solution. His argument was that, of all possible solutions, such a state would best serve Palestinian national interests (that is, he did not consider the state an end in itself, but a means to achieving something more important, something with more worth). At the time, I did not see the value of his proposal. The idea of a state, in itself, had no appeal for me. Perhaps naively, I protested to Professor Khalidi that there was no need for *us* to create a new state: that all we really needed to do was to demand equal rights as citizens within Israel.

In retrospect, I now realize, or at least suspect, that while Khalidi made his proposal from the perspective of the Palestinian diaspora, my own perspective was, unconsciously, totally "home-bound." He primarily had in mind the entire population of Palestinians displaced from their homeland (including himself and his family), for whom he thought the optimum practical solution was one that offered them a state on parts of their homeland in compensation for not allowing them to return to their original homes. I primarily had in mind a different population of Palestinians, those (including myself) who still lived in the homeland but were to one degree or another disenfranchised by the state that controlled it. His was primarily a population dispossessed of its country; mine was primarily a population dispossessed of its rights in its own country. For Khalidi, *us* meant the Palestinian diaspora. For me, it meant my relatives and school friends in East Jerusalem, as well as the other Palestinians in Nazareth and Haifa and West Jerusalem and elsewhere whose acquaintance I had begun to make after Israel's conquests of 1967 made it possible to reestablish ties among Palestinians living on opposite sides of the so-called Green Line.

But whatever *us* meant to me, I think peace mattered more. In 1977, my final year at Harvard, I was bedazzled by Anwar Sadat's visit to Jerusalem, never mind the nitty-gritty details of his peace deal. I saw the Egyptian president exactly as he portrayed himself in his speech to Israel's Knesset: as having walked, like a magician, right through a barrier or a wall. Although the stunning effect of Sadat's visit later subsided as it became apparent that he had left us (now meaning everyone: the Palestinians, the larger Arab world, as well as all those, near and far, who wished to see a real end to the state of war in the region) in the lurch, yet the political dynamic created by the 1978 Camp David talks sponsored by President Jimmy Carter slowly edged toward an ideological spot where peace could *only* mean some kind of two-state solution. At one point, after I returned home from Harvard and began my career as a teacher, I too came to believe that a Palestinian state embodying our national identity on a part of our homeland would be an optimum solution, or a maximum denominator, for all of *us*—enabling those in the diaspora to return to the homeland, those under occupation in the West Bank and Gaza to become free, and those within Israel to gain full equality with their Jewish fellow citizens. However, that belief did not last. Although I have participated with my compatriots in the struggle for a Palestinian state for much of my adult life, with the apparent breakdown of that project I have come back to feeling, as I did right at the beginning of my political self-awareness (and perhaps still as naively), that there is no absolute need for *us* to have a separate or so-called independent state.

What would a state be for, anyway? For a time I did think that our own state was the only means to achieving what was possible of our rights, both collectively and as individuals. Seeing how restrictive of our growth Israel's military rule was, I came to believe that the only way for us to flourish and fulfill our natural potential was to eliminate that restriction—so that farmers could tend their fields without being harassed by settlers and without fear of their land being confiscated and their trees and crops destroyed; so that teachers and professors could be employed on the basis of their academic qualifications and not their security files; so that people could move and travel freely; so that companies could be established, services and institutions set up, houses and office buildings constructed, and so on, guided only by rules set by the Palestinians themselves, to serve Palestinian interests. And I came to believe, likewise, that the only realistic way for the Palestinian refugees to start living normal, dignified lives was for them to come back to this state and to participate in building it up. Finally, I believed that Palestinian citizens of Israel could only come to be regarded without suspicion as full partners by their Jewish counterparts if and when the national aspirations of the Palestinians were realized in a state *other* than Israel.

Was there anything more to my desire for a state? I think not. Deep down, I didn't yearn to wrap the state that would provide me with all these freedoms in an Arab Palestinian flag! True, I sought the flag as well as the passport; but only as a symbol of my freedom and that of my people, as a symbol of our salvation, not as something valuable in itself. To me, what had, and continues to have, value in itself was the people's salvation from the nightmarish situation they had been living in ever since the 1948 *Nakba*—the forced displacement of seven to eight hundred thousand Palestinians from their homes and from their homeland—when, it is felt, our natural course of history was derailed and sent hurtling down into a dark and deadly ravine. Such salvation would be a precondition for achieving individual and collective well-being, and therefore for achieving peace.

Years later, when the retired Israeli colonel Ami Ayalon and I initiated the grassroots petition we called the People's Voice—an "end-game vision" outlining a two-state settlement—one of the principles in the document was that a Palestinian state would be demilitarized. This clause bothered some of my compatriots: not that they wanted a full-fledged army, but they did want a military show-piece, a brass band. I remember Yasser Arafat also considering an army a necessary constituent of a state. The reason was not that people believed a Palestinian army would, or could, have served any real military purpose. But a military establishment is one of the trappings of nationhood that somehow take on value in people's eyes. Another might be a national airline, whose planes would fly all over the world with the Palestinian flag painted on their tails. Or a Palestinian currency, which would have no independent economic means supporting it, but which *would* have a picture of some national symbol printed on its face.

Such trappings may be thought necessary or important, and being thought so may indeed become so. I am not denying that. But I myself have never considered them to be of value, except perhaps as dispensable accessories. They may also be in the nature of distractions (as may the very political structures of which they could be parts) from the basic vision of what a state is for. To me, given what I wanted from a state, and given the region's existing military (im)balances, a Palestinian army, however many tanks and guns it might possess, seemed likely to be totally useless, whether as an instrument of defense against neighboring states or as an instrument of attack against those states, and thus to be a waste of money and effort. Why, then, have an army at all? Why not spend the money on something more directly addressing what a state is really needed for, such as health and education or the more general well-being and dignified living of the people? For me, therefore, the clause in the People's Voice that defined the Palestinian state as demilitarized expressed a Palestinian interest much more than an Israeli "security requirement."

But if, back then, I had come around to the idea of a state because it seemed the only practical means for my people to achieve peace and salvation, since that time the diminishment, through Israeli confiscations and settlements, of the land on which that state could have been established has slowly pulled me back to my original position. After nearly half a century of Israeli rule, the term "occupation," with its implication of an imminent reversion to the status quo ante, has ceased to have real political or legal significance. Since the state, as we had conceived it, is no longer practical or realistic, why keep clinging to it, or to the concept of occupation—especially given that I have not fallen victim to the enchantment of red-carpet trappings or Sirens along the way? Again, what would the state be for?

The natural rejoinder to that last question is another question: What else is there? For self-evident reasons that I will not repeat here, surrendering completely—packing up and leaving the country en masse—is not an option. Staying put, on the other hand, may or may not lead quickly or directly to a one-state solution with Jews and Arabs being equals under a democratic and secular law. So what can we do, or rather what should we brace ourselves for, in the meantime? In asking this question I am seeking an answer which will address the existing reality—a reality defined by Israel. Of course, we can imagine a different reality, in which we could propose other mathematically conceivable solutions, such as a bi-national democratic state or a federation or confederation of city- or region-states. But if we are facing an obstinate occupying power which is impervious to any such solution, perhaps we need to think of proposals that may work as shock therapy to awaken Israelis to the inhumanity of continued occupation, or that may provide halfway measures to reduce, as much as possible, the occupation's deleterious effects on our daily lives.

In recent months Israeli officials, including Prime Minister Benjamin Netanyahu, have declared that Israel is and should continue to be a *Jewish* state, and that it wants to be recognized as such by the Arab world. To safeguard that Jewishness, some officials, including the foreign minister, Avigdor Lieberman, have gone so far as to suggest redrawing Israel's borders to exclude areas with concentrated Arab populations. Much of the Israeli public also wants Israel to be Jewish. However, differences of opinion arise when the question of democracy comes up: many right-wing politicians argue that democracy can and should be ditched if and when it is perceived to endanger the Jewish nature of the state. Others, notably former defense minister Moshe Arens, have proposed that, discounting Gaza and its population, Israel could still maintain its Jewishness even if it were to extend citizenship to the Palestinians living in the West Bank, including East Jerusalem. (As an aside, I must say I find this particular proposal amusing coming from Arens, the man who back in 1991, in his capacity as Israel's minister of defense, signed the order for my arrest as a supposed Iraqi spy and a danger to the "security of the state and the physical and spiritual well-being of its citizens.")

This may turn out to be the single most controversial issue Israel will face in the near future. But given that in 2009 Israeli voters elected a right-wing government, and that Arens's suggestion has attracted neither Israel's right wing nor its left wing—which insists on two states and dismisses the "right-wing one-state solution" as apartheid whitewash—it appears very likely that the current grim reality will continue, with Israelis and Palestinians living as sworn enemies under the same "roof," in an extremely tight geographic space with limited natural resources, the oppressor always in fear, the oppressed constantly squirming to be free.

What scenario can Palestinians, or the otherwise feeble international community for that matter, propose under these circumstances? If neither two states nor a secular and democratic single state is a realistic possibility in the foreseeable future, can we devise some other measure to break the current deadlock while keeping those two options open? As a thought experiment, I will now propose a measure that is so objectionable that it might well generate its own annulment, either by making all parties see the need to find a tenable alternative or, if indeed adopted, by serving as a natural step toward a single democratic state.

In this spirit, then, and as a way to move beyond the seemingly interminable status quo, let me pro-

pose that Israel officially annex the occupied territories, and that Palestinians in the enlarged Israel
agree that the state remain Jewish in return for being granted all the civil, though not the political,
rights of citizenship. Thus the state would be Jewish, but the *country* would be fully binational, all the
Arabs within it having their well-being tended to
and sustained. Given Israel's demand to be recognized as a Jewish state, and as long as it refuses to
grant those Palestinians full citizenship, their next
best option is to have full civil rights even without the right to hold elective office—so that they
can enjoy the civil benefits of the de facto single
state without being accused of diluting or "defiling"
its Jewishness. In any case such a scenario would
provide them with a far better life than they have
had in more than forty years under occupation or
would have under another projected scenario: Israeli
hegemony over scattered, "autonomous" Palestinian
enclaves. (Incidentally, Palestinian refugees in Lebanon have recently, after so many years there, taken
to demanding civil, as opposed to political, rights in
that country. But their situation is not parallel to
that of Palestinians in Israel. While the Lebanese
are reluctant to grant Palestinians political rights,

the Palestinians do not want those rights in Lebanon anyway, believing that the proper place for them to have such rights is in their homeland, Palestine itself.)

There is another angle to this: Palestinians, just as much as Israelis, need to think deeply about what states are for. The utilitarian function of states—as means to enhance human well-being rather than to fulfill jingoist or religious imperatives—needs to be brought to the forefront of their political consciousness. Reflecting on that function, which underlies my proposal, may make them less likely to reject such proposals out of hand. At the end of the day, states must exist to serve the people, not to rule over them. If the international community remains unwilling to challenge Israel's continued rule over Palestinians and possession of the lands that once were designated as a future Palestinian state, surely the least it can do is to insist that Israel provide those Palestinians with full civil and human rights throughout "its" territories, however it has come to possess them. To Palestinians for whom a state of their own has an intrinsic value, the idea of accepting certain rights without full citizenship will be repugnant, even if proposed as an interim arrangement. Likewise to Jewish Israelis for whom the state has an intrinsic value, as well as those for whom it has an extrinsic value as a necessary means to an end such as a place of safety for the Jewish people, and for those who believe the Jewish state is part of a larger divine plan. We Palestinians do not view a national Palestinian state as part of a divine plan; ours is primarily a down-to-earth affair of longing to live normal lives in our homeland. From a purely utilitarian perspective, therefore, if we were granted all the civilian rights needed for a normal life—if, in other words, the State of Israel, backed by an international guarantee, provided the human well-being for which, otherwise, we might have to establish a separate national state—then what need would we have for such a state? Granted, in this scenario we would be excluded from all the rights and functions directly connected to the state itself, such as electing or being elected to the Knesset or other official positions or serving in the army or in government posts. But even without such privileges life under this scenario would be far better than life under continuing occupation or in Bantustans under Israeli hegemony. And why, either in this thought experiment or in a more strategic sense, would we need those rights and functions anyway? Indeed, why should we wish to run the services (security, the economy, and so on) that a state is charged with running? Far better, surely, to allow others to do all this for us—especially if they are dying to do it.

Dying to do it. This sounds like a macabre play on words. But during the period after 2000, when Palestinian suicide attacks almost became the norm to express resistance to the occupation, disaffection with politics, or simply frustration and anger with life itself, I began asking myself what the state we were fighting for is worth. How much killing can a group suffer or commit before the suffering and the loss of life outweigh the values on whose behalf the killing is being committed—before the situation reaches the point of tragic absurdity?

I was, and am, not only thinking of the human death toll of one-time horrible events, like Palestinian suicide attacks in the midst of civilian congregations in Tel Aviv or Haifa, or like Israel's massive and merciless invasion and bombardment of Gaza, events one always hopes one has seen the last of. Contemplating bloody confrontations between Arabs and Jews such as the one in October 2009 near the al-Aqsa Mosque in the part of the Old City of Jerusalem that Israel occupied in 1967, I dread what an increasingly radicalized future may bring. I ask myself: Is violence in that supposedly holy spot, or in its name, whether in attempts to seize control of it or to defend it against a takeover, in any way worthy of the blood spilled? The question is particularly grim because, however hard I try, I cannot foresee such events fading into the unrepeatable past. Quite the contrary, I feel compelled to extrapolate to a future reality in which all the surrounding surfaces seem to be fast closing in toward one another, about to crush everyone inside.

Ruminating about that physical spot in Jerusalem, so revered by Muslims, Jews, and Christians, I wonder which matters more: history or its moral lessons. In other words, I wonder whether it really matters, morally or from God's point of view, which of his sons, Ishmael or Isaac, the Patriarch Abraham set off to offer in sacrifice, and where he set off to do this.

Hence this book. This is not an academic study. It is a set of reflections arising from my lifelong engagement with a seemingly intractable human conflict, one in which I, as a Palestinian living in Jerusalem, am both victim and protagonist. In the chapter titles I pose some of the questions that have haunted me in recent years; in the chapters I try to explain, to myself and to the reader, the ramifications of these questions. I begin with the seemingly simple question of what led up to the current conflict, or how we got into this mess. ("Seemingly" simple because history as a causal sequence of events is far more clouded and murky—even after all the official documents have been released and studied—than we often think.) In later chapters I try to tackle the pressing questions. The tension created when historically motivated actions come into sharp conflict with human values, as in the decision to expel Palestine's Arab inhabitants. The meanings of citizenship, identity, and having or belonging to a state: for example, how Palestinians manage to be both citizens of Israel and its national enemies. What it means to identify oneself as belonging to a party, a nationality, a community, or a group: for example, whether it is conceivable for someone who identifies himself as a Hamas activist to reconcile with someone who identifies himself as a Zionist, and vice versa. What the outcomes of the present situation might be, with or without a successful negotiation or political intervention: for example, whether we can expect the status quo to continue. What determines how we (human beings) act and how we negotiate: for example, how rational we really are. And finally, whether any light is visible at the end of our long tunnel, and what we might do to draw nearer to that light—a question having to do with the roles vision and faith can play in the making of history.

Having chosen education as my lifelong career, and having been administratively engaged in the building of Jerusalem's al-Quds University for the past fifteen years, I also take the opportunity here to reflect on what I believe education is meant to do, and on what it can do for the next generations of Palestinians. I have always thought of education as being in itself an act of liberation, both for individuals and also, in our oppressed circumstances, for the people as a whole. In situations like the one under which we live, I see the student population as the best agency for political change—whether the issue is oppressive rule by another nation or by a home-grown authoritarian autocracy. For me, then, education is more about self-rule than about jobs. But is that why students come to the university, and can part of the "establishment" ever really succeed in sowing the seeds of its own replacement? In all, this book has more to do with trying to articulate questions than with providing answers.

1

How Did We Come to This?

It is hard in the best of circumstances to fully understand or explain the causal flow of historical events, what "truly happened" in a historical episode, or how one episode is linked with or gave rise to another. My aim in this chapter, therefore, is simply to recount what many of us consider to be the known surface facts about the history of the Israeli-Palestinian conflict, thus introducing readers unfamiliar with our region's history to some of the main steps that have led to the current impasse, in which all avenues to peace seem to be blocked.

If it is possible to point to a beginning at all, it can be said that the seeds of today's conflict were sown at the end of the First World War, when the victorious European Allies carved up the defeated

Ottoman Empire. Some of the Arab territories formerly under Ottoman rule became newly independent nation-states. One that did not was Palestine, whose borders, as defined by Britain and France, included both the east and west banks of the Jordan River. In 1922 the League of Nations granted Britain's request for a "mandate" over this region. As part of the Allies' postwar arrangements with local Arab rulers, Britain promptly transferred its authority over the eastern bank to the Mecca-based Hashemite clan, which established the Kingdom of Trans-Jordan. The western portion, which remained under direct British governance and came to be known as Mandatory Palestine, has been the site of conflict from that time until our own day.

Mandatory Palestine, according to most counts, had an Arab population totaling almost half a million people.[1] Some Jews also had been living there for centuries, as they had throughout the Arab world under successive Islamic caliphates.[2] Until the collapse of the Ottoman caliphate, and with the exception of some two hundred years during the Crusader period (1095–1291 C.E.) when Jerusalem was raided and ruled by Saxons and Franks, the region had been under Muslim rule since 638 C.E.

During those centuries the Islamic world encompassed a rich mosaic of ethnic groups and religious communities: Greeks, Italians, Turks, Armenians, Syriacs, Egyptian Copts, Moroccans, Persians, and others integrated themselves into the region and became indigenous to it. There was also a long-standing community of indigenous Christians descended from their religion's earliest times, who had become culturally, linguistically, and politically "Arab" even before the advent of Islam.[3] All these groups, in their rich variety, inscribed their respective histories on the region; their rootedness here, and their cultural contributions, cannot be denied or discounted. Furthermore, in contrast to our own "states-divided" world, their members were dispersed throughout the caliphate's borderless dominions, and travel or migration from one of those dominions to another did not require passports and visas and proofs of nationality (although travelers perhaps had other, more serious problems to contend with). Whether under the caliphate, under its predecessor the Byzantine (so-called Eastern Roman) Empire, or as far back as the time of King David and even before, it is quite likely that, on the whole, the populations that inhabited those regions continued to do so, remaining spread around the same overall geopolitical space.[4] That would change after the British took charge.

In 1917 the British foreign secretary, Lord Balfour, issued his famous Balfour Declaration, promising to establish a homeland for Jews in Palestine. At that time, Jews in the region numbered only a few ten thousands, even though their indigenous numbers had been augmented, beginning in the late nineteenth century, by migration from European countries. The Jewish immigration was fueled partly by rising anti-Semitic sentiment in Europe and partly by the newly emergent ideology of Zionism: the movement to create a Jewish nation-state.[5] Another factor contributing to the immigration was British policy itself, which during part of that period banned Jews from entering Britain while allowing a certain number of them to head for Britain's ward, Palestine.

Palestinians (specifically the Arab population, Muslim and Christian, living in Mandatory Palestine) immediately protested against the Balfour Declaration. Under the Ottoman political system and even earlier, the Palestinians had had an organized local leadership hierarchy centered in Jerusalem.[6] They had also had an active civil society. A telling point is the Palestinian Women's Organization, which was sufficiently nationally conscious to be at the forefront in leading demonstrations, initiating petitions, and generally mobilizing the population against Balfour's intrusive designs.[7] For the region's indigenous inhabitants, the idea of turning their ancestral land into a "homeland" for people from foreign countries (not primarily for the indigenous Jews, who were already at "home" in Palestine), had no appeal whatsoever. Furthermore, its proposal by an imperial foreign power recalled the Crusaders' conquest of the region, reawakening old fears and resentments.

The story was probably different for Palestine's indigenous Arab Jews, who understandably may have sympathized with their European brethren because of their shared religion and shared concern about Europe's anti-Semitism. Many of them joined the war effort against the Ottomans, and at the end of the day Zionism succeeded, on the whole, in winning over Arab Jews to its ideology. In the eyes of their fellow Arabs, this transformed them from neighbors and natural inhabitants of the region into a fifth column serving imperialist European interests. To a large extent, this image still lingers: many Arabs view Israel as an enemy less in its capacity as a *Jewish* enterprise than for its suspected role as a *foreign* enterprise serving western imperialism.

It is important in this regard to point out a curious alignment of historical facts, resonant in people's minds in this part of the world, whose significance will presently become clearer: Britain's deep involvement in the dismantling of two Muslim dynasties—the Ottoman caliphate in the Middle East and, some two hundred years earlier, the Mogul dynasty on the Indian subcontinent. In both cases, Britain, as an imperial power, is viewed as having deliberately destroyed Muslim political structures that extended across vast geographical areas with diverse populations, replaced those systems of government with its own rule, and finally purposefully steered the two areas into partition, with the aim of weakening the Islamic world. This pattern seems all too familiar when one considers what has happened in recent years to Iraq, another portion of Britain's territorial booty from the First World War.

The Allies' defeat of the "Sick Old Man of Europe," as Turkey was called by its would-be enemies, drew a final curtain on the last Muslim caliphate. Several aspects of British policy during the war would later foster conflict in the Middle East. To aid their war effort against the Ottomans, the British established an all-Jewish military regiment in Europe[8] and also mobilized tribal Arab ruling elites (including the

Hashemite clan, descendants of the Prophet Muhammad). To gain the tribal rulers' support, Britain appealed to their natural hunger for power and leadership, promising them rule over independent national states and kingdoms after Istanbul's collapse. Mobilizing popular support for these separatist sentiments did not require much effort, given Istanbul's poor treatment of the provinces in its empire in its final years. Palestinians had sometimes protested Ottoman rule: once in a famous uprising led by Jerusalem's leading families in 1701, during which fresh army contingents had to be dispatched from Istanbul to storm the sealed gates of Jerusalem's Old City. For various reasons, including the caliphate's waning influence in the provinces, increased national self-consciousness among Arab elites, and the able efforts of such charismatic military leaders as T. E. Lawrence, Britain was able to garner Arab support for its war against Turkey. Although Arab history books refer to that period as the "Arab awakening" and the "great Arab revolt," one day Arab historians will surely reappraise those events, questioning whether Arab leaders at the time were truly national heroes or simply tools in the hands of the Allies.

After the war, Britain and France divided up the

conquered territory, arbitrarily drawing national borders to create the new kingdoms and states. They kept some of those areas (such as the Palestinian and Arab Gulf regions, known at the time as Mandatory Palestine and the Trucial States) under their direct control, while allowing others (such as Iraq, Saudi Arabia, and Trans-Jordan) symbolic sovereignty. Syria was first "given" to a member of Mecca's ruling Hashemite clan, then quickly repossessed by France, initiating years of turbulent imperialist rule that would be terminated only when, in the Second World War, British troops invaded Syria to fight what by then were the (pro-Nazi) Vichy government's forces.

Needless to say, a major concern for fast-industrializing Britain and France was to secure control over the area containing the largest known reservoirs of oil and natural gas in the world. If they valued the Trucial States for the oil lying beneath the ground, they valued Mandatory Palestine for multiple reasons, including Christian Europe's lingering desire to have a say in the Holy Land and political Europe's wish to solve its perceived "Jewish problem" at home by identifying a distant geographical space for the Jewish people—a desire which coincided with that of leading Zionists, who lobbied Britain to promise Palestine to *them*.[9] Thus, while Britain turned over the territory east of the Jordan River to the Hashemites to become their "independent" Arab state (the Kingdom of Trans-Jordan), the territory west of the river (Mandatory Palestine) remained under direct British rule until the end of the Second World War. At that time Britain turned over its mandate to the United Nations, which established a special commission to study the matter of Palestine's future. In November 1947 the U.N. passed a resolution favored by a majority of the commission's members, which partitioned the area into a Jewish state and an Arab state while maintaining a special status for Jerusalem.[10]

Britain's final withdrawal was scheduled for May 15, 1948. On May 14, Israel declared its independence. Armed conflict immediately erupted, much of it initiated by the poorly organized Arab leaders in Palestine and farther afield. By that time the Zionist entity was firmly established, its military beefed up by veterans of the British armed forces with experience and equipment acquired in two world wars. Battles between its troops and various Arab armies and Palestinian popular armed groups led to a truce in 1949 that established what became known as the Green Line separating the State of

Israel—which, thanks to those battles, had come to occupy a much larger territory than that allocated to it by the U.N. resolution—from its neighbors: Egypt, Jordan, Lebanon, and Syria. It also separated Israel from two areas that would not fall under Israeli control until the June war of 1967: Gaza, which was ruled by Egypt, and a swath of land west of the Jordan River which was soon annexed by Trans-Jordan. These two areas, Gaza and the West Bank, which constitute only about 22 percent of Mandatory Palestine, are the land on which, for the past twenty years or so, Palestinian leaders have been struggling to establish their state.

Two major Muslim-ruled empires, that of the Moguls on the Indian subcontinent and that of the Ottomans in the Middle East, were both inhabited, for centuries, by ethnically and religiously diverse populations living under single political systems; both were conquered (at different times) and ruled by Britain; and both found themselves, when Britain finally relinquished its dominions after the Second World War, heading straight for partition. The parallels between British policies in India and in Palestine in that period are striking—although while Britain positively sought partition in one case, its intentions were less clear in the other. In *The Last Durbar,* her highly readable account of the last days of "British India," Shashi Joshi portrays the British viceroy, Lord Mountbatten, as trying to persuade the leaders of the various ethnic and religious communities to remain united under one government.[11] Only after concluding that he cannot, in particular, get the Congress Party to agree to work with the All-India Muslim League, does Mountbatten recommend dividing the subcontinent, much to his own disappointment. Historians disagree about whether partition came about through an aggregate of connected but independent acts by individuals or through a process predefined by the natures of conflicting ideologies in which individuals were mere pawns. But however it happened, examining the paths to partition in these two regions may help us understand whether we as individuals can truly make a difference to the world we live in, or whether our impact on history is negligible in a world whose players are much larger than ourselves.

There are three immediate reasons why events on the Indian subcontinent are relevant to our discussion of Palestine. The first, also described by Joshi,

is a politically unconventional proposal reportedly
made by Gandhi just a few months before his assassination. As an attempt to persuade the leader
of the Muslim League, Mohammad Ali Jinnah, to
support the plan for unity, Gandhi proposed offering him the premiership of a united India in return
for certain guarantees of ethnic and religious parity.
This proposal, along with Gandhi's philosophy of
using nonviolence to shape an antagonist's identity
and behavior, will come up again later in this book.
The second reason is the striking resemblance between the two cases in establishing political boundaries on ethnic or religious grounds in regions with
mixed populations. Both Pakistan and Israel, as
products of partition, are self-conscious political
models based on such grounds, with Pakistan having sought to become an Islamic state and Israel a
Jewish state. Even after the major population trans-
fers and the bloodbaths accompanying the two par-
titions, both regions remain major question marks;
it is not at all obvious whether either of them will,
or should, remain divided that way. The third reason is the recommendation made by Nehru's India,
which had been separated from Pakistan two years
earlier at great human cost, to the U.N. commission
on Palestine's future: India, together with Iran and

Yugoslavia, suggested a federal form of government rather than partition as a solution to the communal conflict in the former Mandatory Palestine. In view of changing realities and perspectives since the mid-twentieth century, such a solution may well be worth revisiting.

In Palestine, although the Arab population's resistance to Britain's declared plan to create a homeland for Jews began with nonviolent protests, such as the aforementioned women's demonstrations and conventions and a general strike by Arab workers in 1936–1939, these efforts soon gave way to armed skirmishes and then to real battles, as Zionist Jews pursued their goal of establishing a state, and as Palestinians, with support from their Arab allies, sought to retain their homes and their way of life.

As a way to understand the political vicissitudes of those years, one may tentatively suggest that while Zionists were systematically and positively *acting* to implement their vision of a Jewish state, Palestinians were impulsively and defensively *reacting* to situations imposed on them: not only to the Zionist project but also to their having been left out when the European Allies granted their Arab brethren new nation-states. Palestinian leaders fell far short of acting in the people's best interests, neither making a proper assessment of the challenge they faced nor putting the national interest above their own petty quarrels and personal ambitions. Political party leaders during those years seemed to be—as perhaps it is in the nature of party leaders to be— more intent on achieving power for themselves than on bringing about what was best for the people. The disaster which eventually befell the Palestinians, the *Nakba,* was as much due to these leaders' misman- agement and bad planning in the face of Jewish de- termination and well-planned designs as it was due to the military and political impotence of the newly established Arab fiefdoms.

In view of the three reasons mentioned above for invoking the case of the Indian subcontinent, and considering the political stalemate plaguing our re- gion today, it may be helpful to speculate about how a more peaceful course for Palestine might have been charted. To begin with, the notion of partition, favored by the majority members of the U.N. special commission, might have been better replaced by a federal solution, as recommended by Nehru's India. Some important voices within Pal- estine, especially Jewish organizations such as Brit Shalom (Covenant of Peace, founded in 1925) and later Ihud (Union, founded in the 1940s and represented by such prominent intellectuals as Martin Buber and Judah Magnes), argued in favor of some form of federalism or binationalism on both practical and moral grounds.[12] Such voices did not, unfortunately, find resonance in the largely Zionist-driven Jewish population, nor yet in the nationalist-driven Palestinian leadership. The latter, especially the Mufti, Haj Amin el-Husseini, seemed bent on getting Britain to replicate in Palestine the deal it had concluded with the Hashemites in Trans-Jordan, failing to bear in mind Palestine's distinct historical, ethnic, and religious constitution or the distribution of forces in its political terrain.

Suppose that, instead of taking that position, Palestinian leaders had accepted the first British proposal, adopted by Parliament in 1939, for a tripartite government of Palestine divided equally among Muslims, Christians, and Jews. This would have been a true example of a Gandhian approach, reflecting the self-confidence necessary to compromise in the interest of communal peace and progress. Alternatively, suppose that these leaders had made a far-reaching proposal like the one Gandhi made to Jinnah, offering to let the Zionists run a united government in return for guarantees of the Arab population's political and civic rights. My point is not that such a proposal would have been accepted, but that the very approach it represents was missing from the political arsenal of Arab leaders at the time, and may be the kind of thinking we need today to chart a way forward. Gandhi's offer to Jinnah conveyed the message that India's unity was far more valuable than Hindu rule, as long as basic equality between Hindus and Muslims (and, by implication, members of other minorities) as human beings was guaranteed. In this respect, Palestine's ethno-religious situation was more akin to India's than to those of the Arab countries being accorded pseudo-independence by Britain and France; thus it might have benefited from an approach more like that of Gandhi than like that of the Sherif of Mecca. The Zionists might have been less determined to establish a separate Jewish state, or might have had less logic to back up that position, if they had been offered the larger share in running the government of a binational state. Consider, in contrast, how much less attractive such a proposal might seem to Israelis today.

And finally, given the consequences of the 1948 war, in which Israel gained far more territory than the United Nations had allocated to it initially, it is interesting to speculate on what might have happened if, on the eve of Britain's withdrawal, the Arabs had *not* declared war on Israel but had instead sought U.N. guarantees for a literal implementation of the 1947 partition plan. Arab armed forces, in any case, were not properly prepared for the war; indeed, those in Trans-Jordan were still under British control.

All these hypothetical scenarios are simply examples of the way "thinking outside the box" may sometimes offer ways forward that are not available if one thinks conventionally. "What if" questions need not be merely useless speculation; they can be helpful as thought experiments, encouraging us to be open-minded about what options we may have before us. They are therefore more about possible futures than about counterfactual pasts. What I am pointing out here is not any particular course of action that might have produced a different historical outcome, but the absence of an open-minded calculative attitude that would have kept people's real long-term interests in mind. Perhaps any single decision would not have made a big difference, but an accumulation of like-minded decisions informed less by petty personal ambition and jingoist passion and more by concern for human well-being might have charted a different, and "better," historical course. Unfortunately, the participants at the time, informed by such petty passions and lacking Gandhian imagination, generally assumed that history could be made or changed only through violence or force of arms, and that such virtues as heroism, patriotism, and courage could only be the characteristics of armed soldiers. These assumptions were, and to a large extent still are, central to both the Zionist and the Arab mind-sets, and they continue to produce devastating results.

The Arab armies declared war on Israel in 1948 and lost. By the time a cease-fire was reached in 1949, Israel had expanded its U.N.-defined boundaries from some 57 percent to about 78 percent of the total mandated territory, and had displaced some seven hundred thousand Palestinians from their homes, thus creating the still unresolved "refugee problem." Anger over this loss swept the Arab world and resulted, immediately or in stages, in the collapse of several pro-western governments, notably in Egypt, Syria, and Iraq, and the rise to power of military juntas bent on revenge and the restoration of Arab pride. Terms like "Arab awakening" and "Arab revolt," often applied to the uprising against the Ottoman caliphate, may be better suited to this period following the defeat of the Arab armies in 1948. These years witnessed the growing impact of secular, pan-Arabist, socialist, and Marxist ideas as well as Soviet influence, and the creation of parties and movements which sought to jump-start the Arab world into modernity. But whether in the newly born Israel or in the Arab nations, the countdown to an eventual confrontation was unmistakable. In a sense, Arabs blamed Israel not only for their armies' defeat but also for their societies' economic, social, and political woes, while Israel played up declared Arab aggressive intentions as a way to consolidate internal Jewish solidarity and to garner international military and financial support.

The two areas *not* lost to Israel in 1948, the Gaza District in the south and the eastern hilltops in the center, including Jerusalem's Old City, came under Egyptian and Jordanian rule respectively. While Egypt did not extend its own sovereignty over Gaza, Jordan did annex the other area, extending full citizenship to its population. The enlarged Hashemite Kingdom of Jordan now comprised Trans-Jordan, on the eastern bank of the Jordan River, plus this central territory west of the river, which came to be called the West Bank. As it turned out, when the long-awaited next war between Israel and the Arab nations finally took place in 1967, Arab leaders, in spite of their bombastic language, were again totally unprepared, and the combined armies of Syria, Jordan, and Egypt again lost, allowing Israel to take control of those two remaining portions of what had been Mandatory Palestine.

But if Israel's victory in 1948 was thought to have eliminated once and for all the only other possible legitimate contender for the land of Palestine, namely the Palestinians, Israel's second victory in 1967 paradoxically allowed that contender to reappear on the international stage. After the 1948 war, Palestine's geography was divided into three parts (Israel and the areas under Egyptian and Jordanian rule), and its Arab people were scattered around the globe, threatened with complete loss of their internal cohesion and their national identity. In fact, political discourse during that period did not focus on the *Palestinian* case against Israel, but on the more general *Arab* case, with some governments (such as Syria and Egypt) taking their language concerning the destruction of the Zionist state more seriously than others (such as Jordan). But the 1967 war brought about the political reunification of the formerly severed parts and the reopening of communication channels between their formerly separated populations, as well as a growing realization that the Palestinians themselves must play the pivotal role in resolving their situation—a realization fostered, in part, by increased political ferment among Palestinian refugees. The Palestinian people, represented by the Palestine Liberation Organization, eventually took center stage, especially after 1974, when an Arab summit held in Rabat, Morocco, recognized the PLO as the "sole legitimate representative" of the Palestinian people. From that moment the long and arduous journey to the Oslo peace agreement began, a journey marked and detoured by civil wars in Jordan and Lebanon, invasions by Israel of PLO strongholds in Beirut, violence, hijackings, kidnappings, assassinations, acts of terrorism, and uprisings. After the cot-death of the Oslo agreement the turmoil and violence continued, as exemplified in 2009 and 2010 by Israel's invasion and siege of Gaza and its bloody military attack on the peace flotilla carrying aid to the Gazans, in which several Turkish civilians were killed.

The so-called Oslo Accords between the PLO and Israel, signed on the lawn of the White House in 1993, were in sum a deformed truncation of the partition resolution of 1947, and of other proposals thereafter.[13] Long-standing and declared Arab and Palestinian intransigence vis-à-vis the various peace proposals, often blamed for failure to reach agreement, may in fact have served the purposes of Israel, which in any case based its strategy on military supremacy rather than on paper agreements. It is informative in this regard to contrast Israel's reactions to two very different moves by the Arab nations: the Khartoum Arab summit of September 1967 (with its infamous "three noes," No to peace, No to recognition of Israel, and No to negotiations), which Israel exploited to the full to attract international sympathy and support; and the Arab Peace Initiative of 2002, which Israel largely ignored. Embedded in the latter reaction is a basic skepticism about the Arab world's peaceful intentions. Indeed, if fear has been at the heart of Israel's decisions, it can be argued that the fear has been, and is, far more of *peace* with the Arabs—which might encourage Israel to let its guard down—than of *war* with them. But it is a sorry matter that Arab leaders have not, on the whole, been clear-sighted enough to perceive Israel's real concerns.

The signing of the Oslo agreement allowed the PLO to enter the West Bank and Gaza in preparation for sealing the agreement on a two-state solution. But when, yet again, such a solution did not come into being, the PLO lost its standing among Palestinians, thus allowing for the rise of its long-time rival, the Islamic movement led by Hamas. The choice between these two leaderships seemed, at one stage, like a choice between black and white: we could either follow the PLO along the endlessly winding garden path of negotiations in pursuit of an illusory earthly paradise while Israel continued to entrench itself in the territories it had occupied in 1967; or we could follow Hamas along a thorny path of fighting and mortal danger, whose earthly results might take more than a lifetime to bear fruit, but with a guaranteed paradise in the afterlife. The more elusive the hope for a negotiated solution appeared, and the more desperate the people became, the less it seemed there was actually a choice for the people to make. Finally, as though through some twisted chemical experiment of their own making but not in accordance with their intent, both societies, Arab and Jewish, simply etched themselves into a frieze, neither able to move forward toward a single state, nor yet to separate into two.

2

What Makes Life Worth Living?

Posing "what if" or counterfactual questions to ourselves, I argued in the last chapter, may help us find ways to handle present-day challenges and to chart a better future. How much has our killing of each other for so many years moved us toward peace? What would it be like if killers and victims had to look each other in the face, one human being to another? We typically think of conflicts as occurring between groups: "us" versus "them," "the Israelis" versus "the Palestinians," "the Arabs" versus "the Jews," and so on. All such groups are made up of individual human beings, but the human face is often hidden from view. In a book about a conflict that has brought so much suffering and so much taking of life, it is well to highlight that human face, if only to see whether we can recognize it!

Consider the three winners of the 2009 Eliav-Sartawi Awards for Middle Eastern Journalism. These awards, sponsored by the American peace organization Search for Common Ground, are named after "two courageous pioneers of the Israeli-Palestinian dialogue": Lova Eliav, who lost his position as head of Israel's Labor Party in the 1970s after calling for negotiations with the Palestinians; and Dr. Issam Sartawi, who was assassinated by a fellow Palestinian in 1983 while working to build the peace process. One of the 2009 winners is a Palestinian peace activist, another an Israeli journalist, the third an Egyptian-American journalist. All earned their prizes for having risen, in their writings, above the dominating wave of violence in the region, reasserting as they did so humanity's face.

The Jerusalemite peace activist, Aziz Abu Sarah, lost his older brother, who was killed by Israeli soldiers during the first intifada (1988–1991). But instead of growing up to be a vengeful militant, Abu Sarah became a crusader for peace. Prompted by his own pain, and reaching deep into his inborn humanity, he managed to cross the border of animosity dividing the region's inhabitants. He attracted the awards committee's attention with an article entitled "A Palestinian Remembers the Holocaust," in which he wrote: "Although it may seem strange for a Palestinian to take time out to remember the Holocaust, I felt it was an important step for me. I needed to connect with the pain of those who suffered, and I needed to go beyond nationality to acknowledge the loss of human life . . . some part of me feared that if I sympathized with 'the enemy,' my right to struggle for justice might be taken away. Now I know this is nonsense: you are stronger when you let humanity overcome enmity."[1] Abu Sarah attended the awards ceremony in the company of his parents and his surviving siblings, who beamed with pride.

The Israeli journalist, Yizhar Be'er, and the Egyptian-American journalist, Mona Eltahawy, were honored for bringing to light another human story, that of Izzeldine Abuelaish, a Palestinian physician from Gaza who, in spite of having lost three daughters to Israeli shelling during Israel's 2008–2009 invasion of Gaza, nevertheless came out strongly in favor of reconciliation and peace between Israelis and Palestinians. He did not allow himself to fall prey to pain and hatred. Be'er called

Dr. Abuelaish "the figure of a modern day Job: a pacifist, a doctor who speaks Hebrew and a human being who continues to speak the language of peace even after his daughters were killed." And according to Eltahawy, Abuelaish "seems to be the only person left in this small slice of the Middle East with its super-sized servings of 'us' and 'them' who refuses to hate."[2] What was being celebrated in these three awards, then, was the triumph of humanity over the darker side of human nature. By some incomprehensible serendipity, in the face of death's visitation, the name "Abuelaish" in Arabic means "the living," celebrating life.

Also consider, in stark contrast to these human and humane faces, the gathering religious storm over the Holy Rock in the part of Jerusalem revered by Muslims as the Noble Sanctuary and by Jews as the Temple Mount. Devout Jews, believing the existing physical structure at this spot will have to give way for their divinely destined temple, are stepping up their encroachment on the site in preparation for that historic day. Meanwhile, Muslims throughout the world are preparing for Armageddon, intent on defending their holy mosques—and in particular the Mosque of the Dome of the Rock—which have been standing on the site for the past fourteen centuries. So Jews and Muslims, acting on religious beliefs and backed up by nuclear capabilities, are poised to engage in history's worst-ever massacre of human beings, over a rock.

Here, then, in the juxtaposition of *life* and *rock,* we find ourselves confronted with two opposite sides of the "problem"—ostensibly the Israeli-Palestinian conflict, but in reality one of the most morally challenging dilemmas facing all of us, whoever we are and wherever we may be. The "life" side reminds us of the value or sacrosanctness of human life in itself, its intrinsic worth. The "rock" side reminds us of the value of what gives life "meaning," the extrinsic value by virtue of which we hold life to be important or to have worth. But what do we mean by life's value, intrinsic or extrinsic? And which side would we—should we—choose over the other?

The moral dilemma is expressed by a character in the apocalyptic film *2012,* released in 2009. In the film's final minutes, with the planet Earth about to self-destruct, and with space ships known as "arks" ready to blast into space to preserve cultural treasures and the few human beings fortunate enough to be aboard, the movie's protagonist, a geologist named Helmsley, tries to convince his fellow passengers to reopen their ark's gates and allow the desperate crowd outside to board. The countdown to total destruction has begun, and the clock is ticking fast. Should the people pleading to be let in—men, women, and children—be left behind to die? Helmsley's main antagonist, a task-oriented bureaucrat from the White House, argues fervently against risking the lives of those already on the ship for the sake of those outside. Postponing lift-off to let those people board, he warns, would threaten the entire launch. Why risk failing to save the human race as a whole for the sake of saving a few hundred people? Helmsley's response is simple: What is the value of the human race we are so intent on saving if its preservation is marked by such a heartless act as abandoning those others to die?

Whether in real life or in make-believe scenes, therefore, we are prompted to ask ourselves a basic question: Is the worth—the value—of human life intrinsic to it, or is its value an additional feature, a meaning without which life would be worthless?

In the film, Helmsley's message is that life's worth consists in its humanity. Without that humanity, as exemplified by willingness to risk one's own life to respond to others' cries for help, there wouldn't be anything in life worth speaking for. For the contending parties in the case of Jerusalem's Sacred Esplanade, it appears that life's worth consists in religious beliefs—beliefs positing the Rock as a mystical point of contact between the human and the divine, dispossession from which renders the believer's life devoid of value. After all, can a Jew *be a devout Jew* and drop the belief in the rebuilding of the Temple? Can a Muslim *be a devout Muslim* and drop the belief in the sacredness of the Rock? Surely it is these beliefs that confer meaning on being a devout Jew or being a devout Muslim, and that therefore *define the identities* of the individuals professing to be one or the other. But then, given the impossibility of both rebuilding the Temple and retaining the Mosque in the same physical location, those individuals are bound, by the definition of their own identities, to consider their lives worthless if, at the decisive moment, they are not ready to offer up their lives for the sake of their beliefs.

Others, both secular and religious, may deem life worthless without freedom or dignity, or without national independence or honor. In the Peloponnesian War, the ancient Greek historian Thucydides tells us, the residents of the island of Melos preferred death to losing their freedom by submitting to the conquering Athenians. Meanwhile the Athenian generals argued that their military strength gave them a right to rule; Thucydides was first to record this "might is right" argument against those who believe that life without the additional value of freedom is worthless. The notion that this value is what gives life meaning—and that without it life would not be worth living—is so commonplace that it even appears as a motto on the state of New Hampshire's license plates: "Live Free or Die."

Martyrdom in the name of God is also a common feature of human history. The Patriarch Abraham himself, revered ancestor of both Jews and Muslims, placed faith in God above the life of his beloved son. Abraham's willingness to sacrifice his son tells us that life does not have intrinsic worth: that it can be sacrificed for a higher cause. But God is not always the cause cited in such cases. Advocates of abortion rights also believe that mere life in itself is not necessarily worthwhile: that, for example, life's *quality* can help determine whether that life has worth or value. Supporters of capital punishment think similarly: that life can be, and in some cases must be, terminated for a greater cause (such as prevention or deterrence of future crime). Proponents of euthanasia believe that there can come a point when a person's life loses its worth, and when it may be best for that life to be—humanely—terminated. The list of examples is long and multifarious. Regicide, infanticide (practiced as a religious act and with the community's general well-being as an objective), preemptive military strikes, targeted assassinations, collateral (human) damage, and suicide bombings are just some of the cases in which people "justify" the taking of life, one's own and/or those of others, by an appeal to a supposedly worthier cause.

Not all the examples I mentioned, however, are in the same category. Regicide, the killing of a despot or king with the intention of improving the well-being of a certain population, seems more akin to targeted assassination (now a recognized Israeli policy), and to war more generally, than to euthanasia. Proponents of euthanasia defend it as a humane act of *mercy*. They argue that "mercy killing" exemplifies what being human, being humane, is all about, and that making a person continue to endure an irreversible state of indignity or pain is not in the least humane. Supporters of abortion rights often argue in the same way if, for instance, the predicted conditions of life for an embryo are "inhuman." In contrast to these reasons for taking life, it can be argued that a targeted assassination is a *merciless* act (that is, merciless toward the person being assassinated). Wars too are merciless. Unlike euthanasia, they are never defended as acts of mercy toward the people being attacked—even if and when they are defended as being "just wars" on some other grounds.

Perhaps one way to think of the distinction, or to think about whether there *is* a distinction, is to compare an altruistic act of self-sacrifice such as stepping into harm's way to save a helpless child with a suicide attack such as the one now known as 9/11. In both cases, the purpose of the act is an ulterior cause; but while we look upon the first as a paradigm of humanity, we see the second as blatant terrorism.

So, in a conflict like the one between Israel and the Palestinians, are we right to identify the human face only with those who rise entirely above the tide of violence, who reject violence even in the defense of life itself, valuing life simply as life? Or can we, sorting through this mixed bag of would-be justifications, manage to identify certain types of action which we feel comfortable defining as humane—as on the right side of morality—even though they involve the taking of life?

Is there, in other words, a middle course we can

take, for example by arguing that general rules have exceptions, and that life's worth is in general intrinsic and only exceptionally may require an external cause? One problem with this approach would be to determine whether, if there are exceptions to the rule, there is a rule for the exceptions. If there is not, then exceptions will vary with the parties that make them, and thus any particular exception will be an unreliable guide to what may morally overrule life's sanctity. And if we accept that situation, then we may as well not treat life as having sanctity to begin with, and we needn't be searching for a rule.

But where might we find such a rule, and what would it look like? A reasonable place to begin searching is the individual, for it is with the individual that everything starts, everything that later may become articulated as a theory or norm: crime of passion, self-defense, just war, and so on. And a reasonable level to begin from is the minimum, the most basic level at which we could possibly find sympathy with the perpetrator, or justification (the emphasis here is on "possibly"). Also, such a rule at the level of the individual should have universal applicability: it should invoke or draw upon a feeling or motivation that elicits understanding (that is, a like-feeling or sympathy even if not consent) from fellow human beings generally, not just from one's own community. Paradigmatically, the envisioned taking of life will be accompanied by pain and grief to oneself, and will be done for the good of the person whose life is being ended, rather than for oneself. The most likely candidate for a rule, given these conditions, is an act expressing selfless love and compassion for the person whose life is to be taken away: "selfless" to exclude self-love, and thus to exclude acts such as killing in self-defense; and "love and compassion" to specify that the killing is being committed for the sake of the person being killed. Mercy killing, as a humane act to end the suffering of a loved one, may well be a paradigm of what we are looking for.

Drawing on human feelings about the task at hand, or on what we might more generally call the "humane imperative," is reliable in ways in which reason or a moral concept like justice cannot be. Take justice, for example. To invoke justice to justify the taking of life can invite debate, both about what one means by the concept itself and about whether the person to be punished according to that concept indeed deserves death or is even guilty in the first place.

Reason, in contrast to human sentiment, famously tells me *how* to think, not *what* to think. It is therefore a less reliable source of consensus, or of common attitudinal dispositions. For example, Israelis and Palestinians can both claim to be guided by reason as one group builds settlements and the other blows them up! Israelis may claim that building a settlement or a cement wall is the rational thing to do, while Palestinians may claim the same justification for destroying it. They will disagree on whether the act in question is rational or not. With love, however, or compassion or care or mercifulness, the likelihood of disagreement over *what an act is* is greatly reduced and possibly even eradicated. A terrorist may not feel sympathy toward a mother who shows care for her child, but he will not dispute the fact that she is showing care. I may not care about the same person or idea you care about; but I will not claim that, given that I do not care, you do not or cannot care either. A terrorist may give a care to (that is, take an interest in) the people or items that you or I care about, precisely because he does not care about them himself.

Human sentiments, then, are a more likely source of common attitudinal dispositions, and therefore acts motivated by them will be more likely to elicit universal understanding. Thus if I understand my enemies (or people belonging to another culture) to be genuinely acting out of mercy or love or compassion toward the person whose life they are taking, I will at least rest assured that the act, as an instance of the rule of exceptions, stands on indisputably humane grounds. I will not necessarily feel the same way if the perpetrators cite justice, given my knowledge that they and I may have different views on what justice is. And I certainly will not feel the same way if they cite some religious belief they hold, or some ulterior human or political benefit.

It is eminently arguable—and is being argued constantly—that there are far more circumstances in which the taking of human life may be justified than the bare minimum I have just identified. Struggles for national liberation and wars against evil regimes stand out as paradigmatic examples. Religious beliefs, national or political beliefs or interests, security requirements, and preemptive defensive measures are also cited as such justifications. However, these are not as immediately convincing as the humane imperative. It is therefore understandable if we are skeptical, and cautious, whenever such justifications are offered.

Besides its value as a persuasive rule of exceptions, the humane imperative, rooted in human sentiments, has the additional advantage of being natural building material for a more general humane system of values to which human beings might aspire. Such a system would be less context-specific than any current system and more universal in its applicability. In a possible world whose inhabitants subscribed to this system, conflicting Israeli and Palestinian "values," which have led to so much loss of life, could be replaced by common human values that would contribute to a better life for both Israelis and Palestinians. Imagine a world in which all pretexts used to justify the taking of human life are rejected, the only accepted justification being the humane imperative.

A moral order based on human values would have a much more solid base than one bound to a context-specific (such as national or religious) narrative. If my values as a Muslim conflicted with my values as a human being, it would make no sense for me to reject the latter in favor of the former, as I am whatever I am (for example a Muslim) by virtue of my being a human being in the first place. This is the way philosophers have historically viewed the world, and this is the basis of our current claims to universal human rights. If Muslims and Jews find themselves killing each other on account of the values they hold as being Muslim and Jewish, then clearly something must be wrong with these values, and it is high time for both groups to fall back on some human sensibility.

The need to do so is all the more compelling if, tragically, the very narratives they draw upon for their self-definitions and beliefs are built on misinterpretation of events which occurred in the distant past. Again, I wonder about history versus its moral lessons. Does it matter, morally, which son Abraham was prepared to sacrifice? And does it matter if one of his sons (and which one) is the ancestor of present-day Jews or Palestinians? Though both historians and laymen disagree on the issue, the claim has long been made that today's Israeli Jews are descended from Jacob, a.k.a. Israel, son of Isaac and grandson of Abraham. Shlomo Sand is one Israeli historian who has dared to challenge this genetic narrative, sparking intense criticism and debate. DNA testing now makes it possible to trace the genetic inheritance of individuals and populations. Suppose that such testing revealed, as some people claim it already has, that the critical population mass of the Palestinians carries the genetic line of the biblical Jewish tribes, while the critical population mass of Israeli Jews is descended from other genetic sources? Would such a discovery matter? Surely it would give the national as well as the religious narcissists among us pause.

The mere possibility that we may be deluded as to who, genetically, we are should make us think twice before killing any "enemy" on racial grounds. Far worthier examples to emulate than Israeli soldiers and Palestinian militants who train for the taking of life are Israeli and Palestinian doctors— from the Arab and Jewish physicians who flourished in Muslim-ruled Córdoba centuries ago to their counterparts in present-day Israeli hospitals— who train for the saving of life, and who see their patients primarily as human beings, not as Arabs or Jews. Respect for and preservation of human life, rather than violation of life in the name of any cause, should be what guides both Israelis and Palestinians in their pursuit of a just peace.

3

What Are States For?

Many people, of course, believe there are causes worth killing for, as well as causes worth dying for. My questions in the last chapter were an attempt to abstract from specific peoples, or specific beliefs, and to see whether I could convince myself, from my perspective as a human being (rather than from that of my fellow Palestinians, with whom I naturally share many sentiments), whether such causes in fact exist, or whether life is intrinsically sacrosanct to the last drop. And if such a cause existed, what would it be? A state? Freedom? Life with dignity? Would it depend on the life of a larger group—be it tribe, nation, or religion—that I identify with? In what sense is such a "larger" life connected with mine? Does that larger life itself need a state in which to subsist or to breathe? What if I found that my own various needs, as an individual, as a political citizen, and as a member of a national group, were satisfied in different, and perhaps even contradictory, geopolitical spaces? What if "my" national state turned out to exclude the part I consider my homeland, thereby leaving some of my needs unsatisfied?

The establishment of Israel created a dilemma of identity and of relationship to a state not only for those Palestinians who stayed within its territory but also for the many more who were forced outside its borders. Consider: at the time of this writing, Palestinians, as Palestinians, do not have a state. Most Palestinians, some seven million of them, have states they live in, even states they belong to (for example, Jordan or Chile), but if asked, they would tell you they do not have their own state. (Ironically, before 1948, Jews would have told you the very same thing.) Palestinians living in the areas under Israeli occupation may be said to be under the aegis of a state—neither belonging to it nor, strictly speaking, living in it. (The so-called Palestinian Authority Territory, consisting of Gaza and the

West Bank, is a curious geopolitical creature, almost like a make-believe princedom closed up in a keeper's cellar, but it is certainly not a state.) Palestinians living in the part of Jerusalem annexed by Israel after the June 1967 war may be said to live in a state (Israel) to which, however, they do not belong. In contrast, Syrians living in the Israeli-annexed Golan Heights also live in a state to which they do not belong, but, unlike Palestinian Jerusalemites, they have their own state as well, namely Syria, to which they do belong, but in which they have not lived since 1967.

Palestinians who are Israeli citizens, though living in a state on their home territory, face even more complex challenges of identity than those faced by their geographically displaced compatriots. Here, for example, a distinction may be warranted between a weak and a strong sense of the verb "to have": Palestinian Israelis can feel they have a state in the weak sense (they belong to it), but not that they have a state in the strong sense (it belongs to them or they own it). They may tell you both that they have a state (though it is not *only* theirs) and that they live in it; if pressed, some may say that while they belong to the country where the state is located, and while the country certainly belongs to them, they do not feel that they really belong to the state itself or that it belongs to them. Others may tell you that they are, or ought to be, the state's co-owners. (Paradoxically, the situation can seem even stranger across the river in the Kingdom of Jordan, where some Palestinians may tell you that Jordan belongs to them as Jordanians, not as foreigners or as Palestinians, but where some Jordanians refuse to recognize these people as true Jordanians.) Then there are those Palestinians, whether in Israel, the occupied territories, Jordan, Syria, or Lebanon, who will tell you that they are simply lost—knowing neither what state they belong to nor what state belongs to them.

All this sounds like a jigsaw puzzle, which is what, politically speaking, it is. The puzzle is well worth trying to solve: not simply to satisfy academic curiosity but, more seriously, to find ways to end the cycle of death caused by such fractured identities. Solving the puzzle requires ferreting out answers to the foundational question of what states are for, what functions they are supposed to fulfill. To begin with, the very dispersal of Palestinians into the various states they live in or under compels us to consider the different grades of attachment people have toward states, as well as the importance of people's feelings about states—and to wonder exactly what, in our psychology as human beings, we *need* a state for. I am here assuming that there is a difference between feeling a need for a passport to travel with and feeling a need to have *one's own country's* passport. The first is an understandable functional or mechanical need. The second involves how attached or loyal we feel to the state which issued our passport, or how included or excluded we feel by that state's ethnic or religious or racial policies. It relates, in other words, to the psychological aspect of our relationship to a state, the part having to do with the various meanings of belonging and of having.

To begin to sort out these complexities, let us consider some of the political statements made by Dr. Ahmad Tibi. Dr. Tibi heads his own Arab Party in Israel and is a member of the Israeli Knesset. In fact, until recently he held the prestigious position of Deputy Speaker of the House. The name Tibi signifies, as many Arab family names do, the village or town the family originally came from: in this case, Taybeh. Taybeh is an all-Arab town within Israel, home to some of the million or so Arabs who are citizens of the State of Israel. Most if not all of these citizens define themselves as Palestinian nationally but as Israeli in terms of citizenship.

Tibi has often been the target of attacks by the Israeli media, and by his colleagues in the Knesset, for being more "Palestinian" than "Israeli." But in early January 2008 the daily newspaper *Maariv* hailed him for supporting legislation obliging airlines to pay compensation to passengers for delayed or cancelled flights from Tel Aviv. In doing so, the newspaper said, Tibi had proved himself to be not a one-issue legislator but an all-around legislator—meaning a genuine Israeli legislator, interested in issues other than the Palestinian cause.

Tibi is on record as strongly advocating the establishment of a separate Palestinian state (he was one of Arafat's advisers), and he is vehemently critical of Israel's discriminatory policies against its Arab citizens. And yet, when asked by an al-Jazeera television interviewer during the same week of January whether, as a way of escaping Israel's discrimination against Arabs, he would accept the annexation of Taybeh to a future Palestinian state, he objected with equal vehemence, even indignation. As a *Palestinian,* Tibi argued in favor of the creation of an independent Palestinian state. But as a *Palestinian Israeli,* he seemed to find the suggestion of incorporating an all-Palestinian town that is now part of Israel into that state almost an insult.

The curious psychopolitical reality that Tibi's position expresses is well worth trying to understand. The interviewer had invited him to discuss Foreign Minister Lieberman's recent call for Palestinians to recognize Israel as a Jewish state. This call had raised hackles among Arabs, as it seemed yet another Israeli demand, after the Arab world had already conceded its readiness to recognize Israel's right to exist. Even that level of recognition, many people felt (and still feel), was too much to ask. In normal international procedure, states are simply required to recognize one another's *existence* as a basis for membership in a political community; they are not also called upon to recognize one another's *right* to exist. Now, it seemed, Lieberman and his supporters wanted to raise the bar even higher, calling upon the Arab world to recognize not only Israel's right to exist but also its right to exist as a specifically Jewish state.

For Tibi, declaring Israel a Jewish state was tantamount to demolishing the ground on which he felt he stood as an Israeli citizen. Defining Israel as a Jewish democracy, he said, was an exercise in futility. In this he made a familiar argument: many Israeli Jews insist that Israel can be both Jewish and democratic, meaning that it can have a Jewish national character but still have equal political rights for *all* its citizens. However, many Israeli Arabs (both Muslims and Christians) argue that "Jewish democracy" can only mean "democracy *for the Jews only.*" A state with both Jewish and non-Jewish citizens cannot be democratic if it guarantees preferential treatment to one of those groups and disenfranchises the other. Thus either Israel is Jewish and not democratic, or it is democratic and not committed to one religion. Given that Tibi's identity as a citizen is rooted in the democratic rather than the religious aspect of the State of Israel, asking him to recognize it as a *Jewish* state is asking him to undermine his own status as a citizen.

Next the interviewer turned the discussion to how democratic Israel really was, and Tibi responded with complaints about discrimination against its Arab citizens. The interviewer then asked an explosive but perfectly logical question: Given this discrimination, would Tibi agree to a territorial exchange which would place areas like Taybeh, his family's original home town, under Palestinian sovereignty?

The immediacy of Tibi's unmitigated rejection of that idea may have reflected the fact that the proposal, in one form or another, had already percolated through the Arab community within Israel, sparking fear and suspicion. That is, Tibi's response may have expressed an already-formed public mood. The myriad underlying concerns and fears that combine to give rise to a public political mood or position are often hidden. Instead, adherents "rationalize" that position, presenting it in a way that obscures the dynamic interaction of its varied sources. The argument Tibi used in the interview was that this territory-exchange idea was clearly part of Israel's sinister and unacceptable plan to trade illegitimate Jewish settlements in the occupied Palestinian territories for indigenous and natural Israeli Arab villages and towns—a plan, he argued, that besides being racist was totally unjust, given that the settlements were illegal and achieved by force in the first place. Perhaps Tibi thought this argument well suited to his venue: a television network with a mostly Arab audience. But his genuine concern about the issue was best expressed by his second argument, which he did not dwell on: namely, that as citizens of the State of Israel, Israeli Arabs had as much stake in the state as Israeli Jews, and therefore that the government did not have the right to cancel that citizenship unilaterally, or to parcel off the territory where they lived, lock, stock, and barrel.

It is a moot point whether these two arguments, the origin of settlements and citizenship rights, are ultimately distinguishable; after all, wasn't Israeli citizenship also, in a way, "forced" on the Arab population? More important is the real concern that lay behind Tibi's byzantine polemic. On the one hand, he was making what he felt was a legitimate demand for the establishment of a Palestinian state. On the other, he was making what he felt was a separate and also legitimate demand that he—whose family was originally from Taybeh—retain his citizenship in the State of Israel. The interviewer, also quite legitimately (if provocatively), was questioning the legitimacy of making those two demands *together*. Was Tibi insisting on a Palestinian state *as a Palestinian?* If so, it made sense to ask if he would accept becoming part (and having Taybeh become part) of the Palestinian state. Or was his concern that becoming Palestinian, in that sense, would deprive him of being Israeli? But how much and in what way was "being Israeli" important to him? For example, was it more important than Israel's lack of democracy, or than his sense of being Palestinian?

Unlike the seven to eight hundred thousand Palestinians who were forced into exile during 1947 and

1948, or the twenty to thirty thousand who were forced out of their villages but remained within what later became Israel (as internal refugees), most of Taybeh's residents managed to continue living in their own homes. It is understandable that people in such a context—seeing the structure of a new, "foreign," state being raised all around their lifelong habitat and, accordingly, engaging in a long and arduous attempt to adapt their lives to this evolving structure—would come to look upon themselves, both as individuals and as a town, as inseparable from that structure. Context gives form to, and sometimes even comes to define, a person's identity. In this sense, it is understandable that Dr. Ahmad Tibi, as an individual-in-context, would insist on his political belonging to the Israeli system (his belonging to Israel as a state), while at the same time insisting on what he saw as a national Palestinian right, the establishment of a Palestinian state.

To understand the complexities of Tibi's (or anyone's) identity, we have to consider its various layers or constituent elements. It was clear in the al-Jazeera interview that Tibi was trying to articulate the synthesis he felt between three components of his identity: his sense of himself as an individual (the private Tibi, so to speak), his sense of belonging to a nation (Tibi the Palestinian national), and his sense of citizenship (Tibi the Israeli). We can view his identity as composed of (at least) these three layers, each seeming to exist semi-independently in its own distinct sphere, subject to quite distinct forces or dynamics. The "nationalist" in Tibi seeks self-determination for the Palestinians in a Palestinian state. The political citizen in Tibi, meanwhile, sees himself as an integral member—and, perhaps paradoxically, even a founding member—of the State of Israel and wishes (and feels it is his right) to remain so; thus he considers it insulting for Jewish fellow citizens to suggest that he relinquish that citizenship and join the Palestinian state-to-be. To make matters more complicated, Tibi's nationality and citizenship components are not co-extensive—and even worse, the state of his citizenship, Israel, not only is at war with the Palestinian nation with which he identifies but (at least in Tibi's view) is based, in its very conception, upon the negation of that nation's existence. This makes it all the more complex for us to understand how and why Tibi gives more weight to the citizenship component of his identity than to the nationality component. And we should not forget another aspect of Tibi's identity: his underlying national attachment to the country itself, the land, as distinct from his national attachment to his countrymen.

Viewing Tibi as an individual-in-context not only compels us to cease seeing him as merely a single person or an independent agent; it also signals to us to put ourselves on guard. In the real world, as we all know, what begins as an innocuous-seeming "context" can acquire a kind of actual existence. Indeed, it can become a kind of higher-order being or entity that is far more dangerous and threatening than an ordinary biological individual. Such a being or entity, be it an ideology or a belief system or a government or a state (to name but a few examples), can come to define individuals' identities, and when it does it often begins to control what those individuals do in the world, up to and including the perpetration of horrors. So powerful can these contextual factors become that the individuals themselves, both in their own eyes and to observers, can seem to disappear in favor of their context. Later in this book we shall return to these higher-order beings or "grand players," the heavyweights in our drama, a curious assortment of ideologies and structures we might call leviathans or meta-biological beings, which often overshadow or even smother the real or natural individuals who make them up.

For the moment, however, let us return to Tibi's context. His unwillingness to relinquish his Israeli citizenship and become part of a separate Palestinian state by no means implies that, if events came to a crisis in which everyone had to bear arms, Tibi would join the ranks of his fellow citizens against his fellow nationals. (As a matter of fact, most Israelis who define themselves as Palestinian would refuse to serve in the Israeli Army even were Israel to allow them to.) But we are trying to understand why many Arab Israelis (including some, such as Sheikh Raed Salah, who are part of the Islamic movement and, unlike Tibi, oppose participation in Israel's political system) might prefer to remain part of Israel in the context of a negotiated settlement in which a whole region would become a separate Palestinian state. We may dismiss here the allegation that their motivation is necessarily malicious—that they wish to remain Israeli citizens in order to overcome or "drown" Israel's Jewish population demographically. This allegation, even if it should turn out to be true of some individuals, is by no means the entire story.

At the same time, the claim that Israeli Arabs have simply come, over time, to feel they "belong" in Israel, does not by itself seem sufficient. True, as

we saw in the example of Taybeh, the historical ac-
cident of having the post-1949 Green Line separating Jordan and Israel fall a few kilometers to its east,
thus making the town part of Israel, created conditions under which the town's residents developed a
sense of political belonging. Finding the structures
(figuratively speaking) of a new, foreign state rising
up all around their native habitat, they adapted, over
time, to fit their altered circumstances and to carve
out a space for themselves within the new political
structures. This "fitting" of oneself, let it be noted, is
not physical (as one already feels fitted physically, so
to speak, to one's family village or home town) but
political. It is on a par with the way immigrant Jews
may gradually fit themselves into life in Israel, or
the way immigrants anywhere may fit themselves to
their host country. In a parallel fashion, between
1949 and 1967, inhabitants of villages and towns
east of the Green Line habituated themselves to being Jordanians, and after the 1967 war they had to
begin habituating themselves to living under Israeli
occupation, neither Jordanians nor Israelis but, perhaps, Palestinians-in-waiting.

Not just this type of "fitting" but another, even
stronger sense of political belonging seems to un-
derlie Tibi's indignation at the idea of separating

his home town (and himself) from Israel. This alerts us that there are at least two distinct meanings of "belonging," depending on the prism through which one views Tibi's relationship with the State of Israel. One meaning is the feeling that he belongs to the state. The other, stronger, meaning is the feeling that the state belongs to him. The latter is almost akin to the feeling that *the state is his*.

Once again, it is important to note that we are not referring here to the territorial aspect, the sense in which Tibi may feel that the land itself, the *country*, is his or belongs to him. That sentiment involves his feelings of national affiliation. Rather, what we are dealing with here seems to be a political sentiment, and within that category, we can distinguish between individuals' feeling that they belong to a state and their feeling that in addition the state belongs to them, that it is *their* state. Not exclusively theirs, of course, but theirs as shareholders or co-owners (although sentiments of exclusive ownership are known to exist both among Palestinians, whether Muslim or Christian, and among Israeli Jews). Feeling that Israel the state belongs to him may well explain Tibi's indignation at the suggestion that he, its co-owner, could by fiat be cut off from it and attached to another political structure—

however paradoxical his reaction may seem given that the other structure represents the national component of his identity.

We shall return to the various senses, as well as the political significance, of belonging to a state later in this chapter. Meanwhile, it is in the second meaning of belonging, the feeling that the state belongs to them, that we may find what makes up the citizenship component of people's self-identity. Arguably, one develops the sense of being a citizen (rather than merely a subject) insofar as one develops the sense of being a co-owner of the state, and of therefore having the right to participate in the decision-making processes that go into shaping that state's identity. This is stronger, as I said, than the feeling one may have of belonging to a state. And both these feelings may develop only gradually, in stages. In normal circumstances, such a political evolution of individuals or groups within a state is healthy and speaks for the state's openness and democratic nature. But it can also be perceived as a deadly threat, if the hegemonic group within the state (now in the role of a leviathan or a subject) wishes to retain its hegemony.

It is in this light that we should probably understand the sensitivity among Palestinians about whether or not Israel is defined as a Jewish state. From Lieberman's point of view, one could say, the aim of such a definition is the maintenance of Jewish ownership of the state despite the rising number of non-Jewish citizens. From Tibi's point of view, one could say, the aim is to break that monopoly of ownership—to make room for co-ownership.

This issue will not disappear by itself. Palestinians' concern for their role in the State of Israel was formally and powerfully expressed in 2006 through what is known as the "200 Intellectuals" document (actually entitled "The Future Vision of the Palestinian Arabs in Israel"), which was signed by leading Palestinian Israelis: writers, professors, public figures. First published as an advertisement in the Israeli and U.S. media, this document created quite a storm within Israel's Jewish community and has since inspired an ongoing discourse or dialogue among Jewish and Arab leaders. Its authors demanded "official recognition of the collective Palestinian Arabs' existence in the State [of Israel], and their national, religious, cultural, and language character, and recognition that they are the indigenous people of the homeland." They went on to call for recognition of Israel's Palestinian population's "rights of complete equality in the State."[1]

It is possible to sum up the document as calling for Israel to be a binational state or a united federation of two states. While the document does not specifically call for the establishment of an independent Palestinian state side by side with Israel, the establishment of such a state does not appear to be inconsistent with the document's political philosophy.

It is hard to deny the legitimacy of these intellectual leaders' concerns and demands. But it is equally hard to ignore Israeli concerns regarding these demands and their implications for the Zionist project. As mentioned earlier, without even counting the more than three million Palestinians in the West Bank and Gaza, let alone the many Palestinian refugees in the diaspora who insist on their right of return, Israel's Arab residents, by some calculations, will make up 50 percent of the population within the next twenty years. Such growth will inevitably put an end to the continuity of the Jewish state in its present form.

I have said that contexts can acquire an existence of their own, turning into meta-biological entities that are both more powerful and more dangerous than the individuals who make them up. Indeed, contexts that are initially harmless can contain seeds that, in the extreme, grow into deformed types of governance. A person's psychological aspect of relationship to a state can be private, or it can be contextual. For example, a Palestinian in the diaspora, if offered citizenship in the country where she is living, may tune in on her private, quotidian needs as she weighs taking on that citizenship against remaining stateless. Alternatively, she may weigh the alternatives before her *as a Palestinian,* or *as a Muslim,* rather than as a totally independent, "private" person. Different psychological shades of meaning at the individual level are multiplied at the collective level, when discourse about what *I* feel and believe turns into discourse about what *we* feel and believe, and when these feelings and beliefs are then projected onto a meta-biological being—such as the state itself, or a political movement—as if that larger entity now has a mind of its own.

A well-known logical fallacy consists in characterizing the whole of something with the characterization we give to its parts, for example saying a truck must be heavy because each of the parts that make it up is heavy. In the case of the truck, we are at least talking about matter (metal, rubber, and so on), and about objects that are all of the same sort. But in moving along the garden path from *I* to *we* and then to *the state,* transferring as we move the emotions and feelings of single persons to a group and then to the regime of that group, we clearly must jump from one category of objects to another. This is quite a leap to make. And yet it is precisely along that garden path, or one parallel to it, that we often find ourselves making such leaps—for example, coming to believe that "being Israeli" is inherently and intrinsically "being Jewish" or "being anti-Arab," even when we may have begun by simply expressing a private secular sentiment or a collective but subjective concern about security. In such a metamorphosis, a harmless psychological need for a state felt by individuals may become a collective need, and then may infuse the state with a defining character rooted in that need but grown as a miscreant, in such a way that new generations of individuals become captives of that deformed but defining character. What begins as a normal and justifiable psychological human need thus mutates into a demented ideological imperative or dictate.

One wonders, for example, whether there will ever come a time, assuming continued Arab population growth within Israel, when some Jewish Israelis (collectively) may cease to feel that Israel is their *own* state, their sense of belonging thus becoming diminished. The more Arabs there are who become Israelis, the less Israeli some Israeli Jews may feel the State of Israel has become. To keep it "Israeli," therefore, some may consider it quite acceptable to limit the rights that non-Jewish Israelis can enjoy. Although the parallel is not exact, South Africa under apartheid looms large as an example of what Israel could end up being (or, some argue, what it has already become), with the division between "White" and "Black" replaced by that between "Jewish" and "Non-Jewish" or "Arab." Israel's self-identification as a Jewish state under the present terms means that the more non-Jews there are who are Israeli, the less Israeli a Jewish Israeli may feel Israel has become.

Whether private or contextual, the relationship between human beings (at the individual or collective level) and states or political regimes seems to lend itself to two opposite types of arrangement. The actual state is some mixed form of organizational and normative structures "housing" people or governing their lives. Individuals making up the state may view it essentially and primarily from their private psychological perspectives, as a human project addressing a universal need. Ideally, even as they move on to a stage where they collectively project onto the state their ethnic, political, cultural, and social values, these values will retain their original human content. But in our region, unfortunately, the opposite may happen: the human content may dissolve and be replaced by xenophobic values. There is no better example of this than when, in the name of religious or state security, humanitarian values are flouted, as when innocent women and children are murdered, under whatever cover.

Murder is an extreme form of human brigandry. Less dramatic but equally inhumane forms include robbing people of their basic rights, preventing them from exercising those rights, and simply treating them as less worthy than members of a dominant group. Therefore, as we consider states and the human beings who are housed by them, or belief systems and the human beings who hold them, it is quite possible to envisage a relationship in which the states or belief systems are either so dry and evacuated of organic content or so infused with human characteristics that they take on a life of their own, while either still maintaining human content or—informed by xenophobic values—leaving it behind. In the latter case, states and belief systems may become so reified that they begin to be seen as independent living entities with their own laws of motion, to which human beings are subjected. Indeed, in some contexts the state is so glorified, viewed as so much grander than individuals, that it is no longer conceived as a structure whose purpose is to serve those individuals. Quite the contrary, the relation between the two becomes reversed: instead of individuals "having" the state to fulfill their needs, the state is regarded as primary, as what "has" individuals as its tools, its building blocks, or simply its guests or lodgers.

The question of which has primacy, the state or the human beings, has far-reaching implications. At one end of the spectrum, where the state is the subject, human beings the object, is the image of an Orwellian or Stalinist regime in which individuals are looked upon and treated as mere instruments. In this picture, states are but dehumanized machines. At the other end of the spectrum is a state so infused with human emotion or passion that these feelings are reflected in various forms of overblown self-worth. Here, the emphasis is less on the structure of government than on the ideological constitution of the party or person claiming the state as its own. At the extremity of this paradigm is the image of a self-styled super-race.

Given the daunting characteristics of these two extremes, no wonder many of us believe that life in between offers a far saner prospect! Fortunately, many of us will maintain our sanity and avoid these excesses by reminding ourselves of our private perspective: of what, as individual human beings, we need states *for*. From this perspective, it just seems common sense that states exist *for us*—not in the sense of our owning them as we might own real estate, but in the sense of their being (or of our assuming they are) our extended homes, familiar public spaces, constructed by us, where we feel as entitled as the next person to speak our minds, and where we can expect our general well-being to be attended to and cared for. In this light, the question of what states are for is ultimately about what it is to feel at home, about our inner emotions and aspirations, about who we are as human beings and how we can best live together.

Not that what the state (the structure itself) means becomes less important when we focus on the human content in the formula: quite the contrary, our feelings about how we should be living

together will still, ideally, be defined by human values, however colored by our ethnic or other spe-
cificities. And in the less than ideal situation where
the structures we build are *predeterminedly* exclusiv-
ist, as in the case of Israel, one hopes that means can
be found to bring those structures back to a more
inclusive form. Clearly, it is important to distinguish between what may be considered justifiable
claims by a given "us" on what the state should be,
and claims that are unjustifiable. To distinguish, for
example, between claims that a state be Jewish, that
it be for the Jewish people, that it be the *only* state
for the Jewish people, and that it be for Jewish people *only*.

To return to the Palestinian experience, imagine
that you are a Palestinian asking the grand political
question "What is a state for?" and examining your
feelings about a possible Palestinian state. Perhaps
you are already a citizen of some other state, belonging to that state and enjoying the basic advan-
tages—security, work, education, property ownership, services, and so on—that states are supposed
to provide for their citizens. If so, you may not feel
an urgent need for the creation of a specifically Palestinian state. For you, instead, the most important
felt need may be the opportunity to exercise your

"right of return": to return to your original home, Palestine, now Israel. Or perhaps you are a refugee, or a descendant of refugees, and are not a citizen but a mere resident of a nearby country, such as Lebanon. If so, you may share with other refugees and exiles the longing to be allowed to return, and you also may also wish, in the meantime, to be provided by your country of residence with all the benefits of citizenship short of actual political citizenship, acceptance of which would signal (to others and to yourself) that you have forfeited your right and claim to return to Palestine.

Now imagine that you already live west of the Jordan River, in what you regard as your real country, and hold Israeli citizenship—but that as a Christian or a Muslim, you feel semi-disenfranchised by the predominantly Jewish state, and also feel short-changed as a Palestinian whose people "lost out" to Israel. If so, you may be of two minds. You may wish to be granted full rights as an Israeli citizen, equal to those enjoyed by members of the religious majority, while also wishing for the establishment of a self-sustaining and independent state for your fellow Palestinians who, living in the occupied territories, are not citizens of Israel. Like Tibi, you may not want to move into that new state, nor may you want the Arab areas within Israel to be annexed to it, but you may feel that a state for the Palestinian people would address the national as well as the quotidian needs of your non-Israeli fellow Palestinians, and also that it might aid your own struggle to co-own the State of Israel, which you now feel by right *belongs to you.*

And now imagine that you are one of those Palestinians living in the West Bank and Gaza, the territories occupied by Israel more than forty years ago. You too want the benefits that states are supposed to provide for their citizens, and you also may be of two minds about how to achieve those rights. Perhaps, for a period of time, the need to have your own state, to be free of occupation, seemed pressing, and perhaps you still see your very own state as the natural source of the benefits you crave. At the same time, you may wonder whether a separate state is really the best of all solutions; weighing your *national* desire for a state against your *citizenship* need for a state, you may begin to think that your best course would be to join your fellow Palestinians who are already citizens of Israel by acquiring Israeli citizenship yourself. The state would not, then, be *exclusively* yours: you would share it with Jewish

Israelis. But its geographic space would be the entire country that you feel is yours.

Whichever of these Palestinians you may be,
wherever you may live, in the present situation you
are likely to feel your life is incomplete or defective.
As you network with other Palestinians and attempt
to navigate through the complex political landscape
that surrounds you, you are searching for the best
way to realize yourself as a Palestinian, as a citizen,
and as a human being.

Of course, in any political situation where a question like "What is a state for?" has practical consequences, it is not necessarily considered by every
person affected by those consequences, let alone
considered in the same way. Nor are the conclusions
reached by various individuals typically congruent
or even similar to one another. But the departure
points for contemplating change in such situations
do seem to be similar: the individuals' immediate
life conditions and concerns, such as how well they
feel the state under which they live is treating them
and what changes they feel would improve that
treatment.

Such questions can be posed from both ends of
the spectrum. Just as Lieberman envisions Israel as

a totally Jewish state with Arab population centers carved out of it, some Israeli Muslims see the State of Israel as a political interloper in a country that should and eventually will acquire a Muslim political structure. Elsewhere in that cauldron of contradictions (if I may change the metaphor) are the zealot settlers, who assume they already know what their state is for, but who have an expanded view of its geography and view Palestinians living within it or under it as trespassing on *their* rightful and exclusive public space, and who therefore wish to expel the Palestinians from that space.[2]

What I have called Israel's cauldron of contradictions includes other conflicts and disputes besides that between Jewish and Muslim citizens. Members of the *haredim,* Israel's ultra-orthodox religious community, do not recognize the authority of the Israeli government; for example, they refuse to serve in the army (to the chagrin of secular Israelis). And even this community is divided, as became clear in 2010 when Ashkenazi haredim (primarily of European descent) refused to have their children educated in the same classrooms as the children of Sephardi haredim (primarily of Middle Eastern and North African descent). The state instituted court proceedings against some forty-eight of the Ashkenazi families, sparking widespread unrest and street demonstrations.

In our context, the case of the haredim adds another dimension to the story: being non-nationalist, and in some cases even anti-Zionist, many of them are actually anti-state, biding their time living under the aegis of the state, so to speak, pending the appearance of the genuine State of God, whose arrival they believe will be brought about without human intervention. Their position contrasts quite ironically with that of Dr. Ahmad Tibi, who is not Jewish but is a state stakeholder.

In a land so full of conflicting identities, one wonders what the future holds: further splintering or social healing. Even Palestinians who are Israeli citizens and who, like Dr. Ahmad Tibi, have engaged fully with the system, are sometimes threatened with loss of citizenship and expulsion from the state. A few years ago Azmi Bisharah, a Christian member of the Knesset and a one-time candidate for Israeli president, was accused of high treason and had to leave the country to avoid going to prison. Stories like these keep reappearing. In May 2010, Hanin Zu'bi, a member of the Knesset from Nazareth, was aboard the *Mavi Marmara,* one of the ships in the aid flotilla bound for Gaza. For this action, presumably an expression of the "national" part of her identity, she was later shouted down in the Knesset by fellow members and called a traitor whose diplomatic passport should be revoked and who should be stripped of her Israeli citizenship altogether. Like Tibi, Hanin comes from what we might call an integrationist school of thought (that is, Israeli Palestinians who see value in participating in the political system, as opposed to the Islamicist school of thought, which opposes participation), and from a family that has long been active in the Israeli government. Today she represents, like Tibi and many others, that curious mixture: an anti-Zionist stakeholder in the State of Israel. She ran for the Knesset, but she leaves the chamber when the *Hatikvah*, the Israeli national anthem, is sung. Her vote may be Israeli, but her heart remains Palestinian.

4

Can Values Bring Us Together?

The novelist Amin Maalouf, a Frenchman of Lebanese descent, lived through the 1976 civil war in Lebanon, when the mounting antagonism between the country's ethnic and religious communities, including the Palestinians in the refugee camps, exploded into bloody internal battles. In a perceptive book entitled *In the Name of Identity*, Maalouf argues that human beings always face a choice between defining their religions or ideologies and being defined by them. In spite of having witnessed the total disintegration of human values that these communal, ethnic, or religious associations can cause, Maalouf nonetheless ends the book on an optimistic note, concluding that the humane spirit within individuals can always control the surrounding layers of identity.[1]

Maalouf's insight draws upon a phenomenon which we are fully acquainted with, but whose far-reaching implications we do not always appreciate. One of the early lessons one learns in philosophy is to distinguish between objects and the properties they are supposed to have—a lesson that applies whether the objects in question are trucks or human beings. But one soon learns another lesson as well, namely, that what begin as properties can become, in our eyes, objects themselves, and that these too can come to have properties. In this way, "is a Muslim" and "is an Israeli," as properties of individuals, give way to Islam and Israel; and after just a few more steps along this primrose path, Islam and Israel come to be looked upon as independent beings in their own right, somehow obeying their own laws of motion, and dictating those laws to the human individuals who "are Muslims" and "are Israelis."

It may all begin with initially innocuous identity descriptions: the ways in which we describe ourselves and others and characterize our various affiliations. Here we look at the individual through binoculars, situating her in a specific context and pinpointing her as being part of that context. Her context may be multilayered and complex (for example, she may be, like Dr. Ahmad Tibi and Hanin Zu'bi, both Israeli and Palestinian, or like Amin Maalouf, both French and Lebanese), but the multiplicity or apparent incongruity of these layers or aspects of individuals' identities is not what causes the real problem. The problem arises when one such aspect grows out of all proportion and, transformed from a property to an entity or a being in its own right, begins to control the individual's life. Suppose for a moment that I am that individual. In extreme cases, such an entity or being may compel me (that is, I may *imagine* that it compels me) to commit acts from which I as a human being would recoil. What I, the individual flesh-and-blood Arab or Jew, *ought* to do comes to be dictated by what I believe the abstract but rigidly defined "the Arab" or "the Jew" would do in similar circumstances, or by what I believe rigidly defined "Arabness" or "Jewishness" requires me to do, or even by what someone I trust who claims to speak in that entity's name tells me I should do. And so I, the natural and primary individual, the autonomous human being, become a compliant puppet in that entity's hands.

Or so we individuals may convince ourselves, thus surrendering our wills to the larger entity and

hoping that doing so will absolve us of moral responsibility for our actions. But surely, even after an
abstract entity or cause begins to dictate what I do, I
will not take a particular action—whether evicting
families from their homes or blowing myself up in a
crowded nightclub—unless there is some sense in
which I myself, the individual supposedly of sound
mind, feel the action is what is best *for me*, in particular, to do. I may have participated, with many
others, in the invention of a god (or a cause, such
as Marxism) as an imagined source of my earthly
well-being, and I may perform deeds which I hope
will contribute to my well-being in the name of that
god (or of a cause, such as freedom from occupation). Either way—whether I perceive a cause to
have been born out of a quotidian need or I perceive
an act to have been born out of a cause—there is
a danger that in acting for that cause I may violate
what I know are considered to be basic human values, and there is a sense in which I myself am the
ultimate imagined beneficiary of what I do. Thus
I cannot, in all honesty, absolve myself, or be absolved, of responsibility for my actions.

We do not always appreciate the tragic power of
the spells human beings create and then become
bounded by in pursuit of their own well-being.

Imagine an ancient society developing in a fertile river valley. Its people's well-being depends on successful harvests, but in some years the river overflows its banks and floods the fields, destroying their crops. So contorted in the people's minds does the process of achieving well-being become that they invent a god for the river, a god who causes the floods when angered. Then they seek ways to appease that god to ensure their well-being, and eventually they come to believe that sacrificing the life of a loved one is the price they have to pay. Once this belief nestles into people's minds, they come to accept, however grudgingly, the "need" to offer a child in sacrifice when it is their turn to do so. They may mourn the child intensely and feel they are not responsible for its death because the sacrifice was forced upon them by a higher being—the river god. It would be wrong for us to judge such people formally by our modern standards, for instance by considering them murderers as we understand that term. But surely it also would be wrong to suspend our moral judgment altogether, telling ourselves that sacrificing our children can under some conceivable circumstance (such as on instruction from God) be the moral thing to do, or at least not immoral, and that it is an act for which its perpetrator cannot be held morally responsible. (I will return to a brief consideration of whether there are values in the absolute sense at the end of this chapter.)

The contexts in which individuals are situated, then, such as being affiliated with a belief system or a movement, can be a gateway through which higher-order entities such as man-made gods enter the picture and begin to dominate. On one side of this picture are ordinary human individuals, self-conscious biological organisms who seek their own well-being. On the other side of the same picture, however, assuming that a metamorphosis has taken place and these higher-order creations have taken over, are lifeless layers of structures and entities through which the individuals seek and/or articulate this well-being. As meta-biological *structures,* they may take the form of ideologies, norms, belief-systems, religions, regimes, states, and so on. And as meta-biological *entities,* they may take the form of gods, families, tribes, nations, political movements—in short, anthropomorphized higher-order objects acting as if they belong to the biological side of the picture. But whatever form they may take, they threaten first to dominate and then to dehumanize the real, flesh-and-blood individuals who created them in the first place.

These structures and entities have been sadly plentiful throughout history. But even if, in some earlier age, infanticide (or cannibalism, to take another example) may have been, under certain circumstances, condoned or even considered a moral imperative, in our own age human beings have largely purged themselves of these beliefs. Given history's, or humanity's, evolution, if we encounter such acts in the present, surely we are no longer constrained from passing moral judgment on them or, more to the point, from considering the perpetrators—whether suicide bombers, Nazi officers, or zealots of various causes, to name but a few of the millions of kinds of perpetrators in human history—responsible and therefore culpable for their actions, regardless of what meta-biological excuses they may offer, such as having been required to do what they did by their state or their religion or their cause. Perhaps if responsibility had been duly apportioned in Maalouf's Lebanon in 1976, then in 1982 the Lebanese Phalangists would not, under the cover and with the help of Ariel Sharon's Israeli army, have entered the Palestinian refugee camps of Sabra and Shatilla and brutally massacred men, women, and children.

It is not entities like "the Phalange" or "Israel" or

"Islam" or "Hamas" that are culpable and should be
held to account for any heinous actions committed
in their names, but the individual perpetrators
themselves. If we exonerate the individuals by virtue of their belief systems, we will create even more
room in our world for those meta-biological beings to thump viciously and bloodthirstily around.
Consider the events surrounding what is alternately
(and darkly) called "The House of Peace" and "The
House of Contention," a building in the West Bank
city of Hebron taken over by Jewish settlers in 2007.
In December 2008 the settlers were forcibly evicted
by Israeli authorities, and their supporters went on
a violent rampage. The *Haaretz* reporter Avi Issacharoff tells a grim tale that took place when he and
other journalists covering these events had to switch
roles and become participants to save the lives of an
Arab family of about twenty people after settlers
determined to evict them from their home decided
to set it, and the residents inside it, on fire. No one
else was on hand to defend the family from the
masked men surrounding the house, shouting
threats and hurling bottles and rocks. Arab neighbors cringed inside their own dwellings, afraid to
show their faces in front of the angry crowd. The
army seemed to be on another planet, neither pres-

ent nor responsive to the frantic phone calls made by the foreign and Israeli journalists at the scene. The journalists finally saw no alternative but to jump to the rescue. The family members survived, but their house was destroyed. When the police belatedly arrived to disperse the attackers, Issacharoff heard a voice in the crowd calling them Nazis.[2]

Issacharoff's report is horrifying, even to one, like the author of these lines, who had visited the area a few months earlier and witnessed first-hand the shocking terrorization techniques practiced by the settlers against the neighborhood's Arab residents. This and other rampages against Palestinians in the occupied West Bank, which the Israeli media did not shy from calling "pogroms," sparked outraged declarations from Israelis across the political spectrum, including then-Prime Minister Ehud Olmert himself.

But a question here challenges us: Do individuals who acquire the property of "being a settler" become enslaved by that property's definition, and thereby escape personal responsibility for their acts? In Israel the term "settlers" refers to Israelis, including new immigrants, who have established urban colonies in the territories occupied in 1967, with or without government assistance. According to international law they are illegal trespassers, as are their colonies. Even so, "being a settler," as a description of a particular individual, need not mean "being a murderer" or "being a Palestinian hater," just as being a Phalangist need not mean hating Palestinians, or vice versa. Even in the dreaded Tel Rumeida neighborhood in Hebron, where Arab children walking to school each morning are taunted by Israeli children who hurl filthy abuse at them, and where actual filthy garbage is thrown onto Arab houses from overlooking settler dwellings, and where an entire downtown market street has been evacuated by soldiers, who stand guard to prevent Arabs from entering—even there, in the vicinity of the tombs of the patriarchs, "being a settler" need not divest an individual of human content, turning him or her into an irredeemable thug and murderer. In other words, the individuals behind that acquired property should still be seen as in charge of their own behavior, and can still be called to account for their heinous crimes, not absolved of them. For surely confronting such aberrant behavior and taking corrective action is the only way we can possibly rein in the wild passions in human nature which, even in the name of a higher cause, can make us indistinguishable from brute beasts.

Lest it be thought that in our region the takeover by such meta-biological entities and structures occurs only among Israelis, we have only to remind ourselves of the wave of Palestinian suicide bombings in the few years following the outbreak of violence in 2000; and, even more recently, of the total collapse of order in the Gaza Strip, including bloody clashes between Hamas and Fatah in which bodies were hurled from rooftops and corpses were mutilated, as beastly passions reared their heads, and merely belonging to one or another of those two movements meant that your life was on the line.

The ease with which the tentative first steps are taken to servitude for these entities cannot be overstated. Note how easy it was in the previous paragraphs to move from discourse about individuals to discourse about the larger players (here, Fatah and Hamas), as if it were those meta-biological entities rather than the individuals themselves which had engaged in those clashes. In such cases the individuals fade from view, blocked out by their geopolitical situation or context—those lifeless layers which turn out to be playing fields for entities of an altogether different kind, the "grand players," much larger and more formidable than the natural individuals with whom we started. They are curious entities, these grand players: the State of Israel, Hamas, Zionism, the Palestinian Authority, the Palestinian People, the Jewish People, the Settlers' Movement, the PLO, and others. On the one hand they seem real enough, as if they have lives and minds of their own, undeterred and unintimidated by their individual members or adherents, including the individuals who supposedly run them. On the other hand, these players are not *natural* entities the way human beings are. Rather, they are constructs —created by the natural individuals as institutional mechanisms meant to help run their lives and en- sure their well-being. They are meta-biological, vir- tual, imagined, transcendent—whatever. However we define them, it is hard to imagine that they are impervious to human influence. And yet, instead of being viewed as functional constructs whose raison d'être is the human individual, they come to be re- garded almost with awe and reverence as indepen- dent organisms far more important than the indi- viduals who make them up. No longer viewed as tools or means subject to being designed, defined, and shaped by those individuals, they begin to seem like ends in themselves, and like agents in their own right with power to shape the destinies and the lives of human beings.

It is in this vein that questions concerning political events—for example about whether a Palestinian state will ever exist, or whether its existence would be a good thing—come to be discussed not at a primary level addressing quotidian life, but at a theoretical or ideological level addressing the mysterious forces or grand players of history. It is also in this vein that political discourse comes to be articulated in terms of such questions as whether *Israel* is capable of changing its policy, or whether *Hamas* is an obstacle to peace, as if ordinary human beings no longer matter.

And so we find ourselves trapped between the anvil and the hammer—between biology and meta-biology. On the one hand, the more we abstract the individual from her surroundings, emphasizing her transcendent personal emotions and concerns, the more we risk losing her altogether as a realistic object of discourse. On the other hand, the more we consider the individual from a contextualized perspective, the more we risk losing sight of her and seeing only her various contexts, which are nothing but playing fields hosting the more powerful meta-biological entities, like political parties or religious or national movements, with which she is associated, but which seem to be governed by their own mysterious and independent laws of motion.

Traveling this slippery road to meta-biology can

have far-reaching and dangerous consequences which cannot be overemphasized. Not only may observers or political analysts lose sight of the individual; the individual may well lose sight of herself, coming to see herself primarily through the "eyes" of the larger players. "Being Hamas" or "being Palestinian" or "being a Christian Arab" or "being a diaspora Palestinian" may become such a powerful marker of her identity that she ceases to think of herself—to define herself—except in terms of belonging to that party or movement or category. Tragically, coming to define herself in that magnified way makes the individual lose faith in her ability to control her life. Since Hamas, for example, is such a grand player, individuals who identify themselves so closely with that party, feeling small in contrast with it, come to view themselves as powerless to influence its identity. And since their party's identity is what now defines them, they even begin to see themselves as powerless to shape their own personal lives. Coming full circle, they start believing that they as individuals are powerless to change the world they inhabit—including, therefore, powerless to change what "being Hamas" is. In this self-actualizing process, Hamas, or "being Hamas," comes to be viewed as having a rigid identity, one that is unchangeable, unyielding, bent on a course of action or a role in history, and unstoppable by real-life individuals.

This view of the world is a grim one. The preceding discussion—being as true of Israelis and Jews as it is of Palestinians—can lead us to conclude that the world is like a jungle, or a universe of free-floating rock masses with already-formed, rigid identities and pre-set courses of movement. "Being a Palestinian nationalist" and "being a Zionist" are two such entities, with preformed identities destined to clash with each other. In this world, the individual wakes up in the morning as a Hasidic Jew, a devout Muslim, an Israeli, a male, a settler, a refugee, and so on. In this way, the individual discovers himself (that is, discovers what labels he has pinned on) exactly as he would come upon or discover any other fact of life. As he moves around in the world he encounters other parties or individuals with similarly or differently predefined roles, some who are locked in either as his enemies or as his friends, others whose orbits are so removed from his that he can disregard them. So frozen is he by the identity definitions by which he sees himself and others that he comes to believe he cannot change those definitions to make a better kind of life for himself and others. It is not that he feels powerless to make an impact, to change the world. He may well be able to change the world—but on this view doing so will not mean being able to shape or redefine identities. It will rather mean, inevitably and sadly, simply succeeding at playing his predefined role, at reconsolidating his given identity, at crushing and defeating his predefined enemies, at asserting his categorical ego at the expense of those of others. Depriving ourselves of the privilege of imagining what it would be like to have the power to redefine the world around us, we instead submit ourselves the way we imagine the world has already been defined.

When we as individuals come to define ourselves by these larger entities, perhaps what happens is that we confuse properties we are born with, which are on the whole fairly fixed, such as our gender or color or nationality or mother tongue, with acquired properties such as our political affiliations, and conclude that we are as much bound by the latter as by the former. Such confusion may most easily occur when a property belonging to the first category, such as being born into the Lebanese Druze religious community, seems indistinguishable from a property belonging to the second category, such as being affiliated with a Druze political party. Certainly most of the Lebanese political factions are expressions or extensions of religious communities —some of them, like Maalouf's Eastern Melkite Christians, so small that they may not even be considered separate communities in their own right. Even so, you as an individual can find your individuality, whether as subject or object, totally eclipsed by that contextual association, compelling you either to pick up a gun or to lose your self-respect.

Lebanon is a good example of the way meta-biological entities can be the main actors of political events. It is also an example of the disastrous consequences that can ensue when ordinary individuals surrender their political will to those entities. Individuals allow themselves to melt into population clusters—the Phalange (Maronite Christians), Hizbullah Shiites, Amal Shiites, the Druze community, Sunnis, the Palestinians. Were one to view Lebanon as a transparent sphere containing six different areas representing these six clusters (the number is in fact much larger), and were one to assign different colors to those clusters to identify the different political alliances between them, the result would be a constantly changing color-map. Tragically, changes reflect the power games of ruling cliques rather than true ideological differences. My being a Druze may one day mean my being anti-Syrian, but the next day it can easily mean being pro-Syrian, if the power games played by my leader so dictate.

The consequences of these power games are tragic. They are tragic of course for the Lebanese people. But they are equally tragic for the Palestinians. Indeed, of all Palestinian communities, the hundreds of thousands of refugees living in Lebanon may have paid (and still be paying) the highest human cost of the *Nakba:* here, even more than under Israeli occupation, the Palestinian tragedy is exhibited in its true colors. The pitiable conditions of the refugee camps today stand in grim testimony to the bloody and political vicissitudes faced by a segregated refugee (predominantly Muslim) population in an already precariously balanced political system. On the one hand the refugees are denied basic jobs and civil rights in that system; on the other they pose a destabilizing threat to the system's very existence. Factional alliances, always shifting in the power games of the grand players and those who claim to be their spokesmen, have expressed themselves in violations of human rights, acts of vengeance, and atrocities such as the Phalangist massacre of hundreds of Palestinian men, women, and children in the Sabra and Shatila camps in Beirut in 1982 as well as the earlier internecine atrocities of 1976. When clashes take place between the grand players, individuals are automatically stripped of their personal identities, so to speak, and seen as indistinguishable instances of the larger group, whose bodies can be cut to shreds—not because of who they are as individuals, but simply because of their belonging to the larger group which has taken them over and is now on the battlefield.

Group identity need not always blot out personal identity or drive people to such extremes. Indeed, Fatah and Hamas can co-exist as well as fight, as can Lebanese Shiites and Palestinian refugees. But it is almost common political wisdom that contending groups will fight until they establish a hierarchical order of power. On this view, political entropy thrives where a resolution of power is absent, and stability and order will prevail only if the balance of power is maintained. Maintaining that balance may come at a cost: for example, the ruling group may have to quash skirmishes or insurgencies or rebellions, which may hurt, but will not topple, the existing order. Better that constant need to keep the lid on the situation, decision makers are told by their political or military advisers, than entropy or the risk of being overcome by the other side.

The main flaw in this supposed wisdom is the absence of history's human face. When we accept this account as is, we soon find that we can no longer distinguish between right and wrong; right is simply might, as Thrasymachus argues in Plato's *Republic* and as the Athenian generals try to convince the islanders of Melos in Thucydides' *History of the Peloponnesian War*. History's human face— that face of forgiveness and commitment to peace which manages to transcend the individual's tragic context—simply disappears.

Considering this matter of right versus might, we can distinguish at an elementary level three possible ways of thinking about what we normally understand by "right," or human values. One (let us call it idealistic) account asserts the existence of such values—for example, norms associated with religious beliefs—but proposes them to be Platonic, that is, to belong to (have their meaning expressed in) a supra-human order which preexists and is separate from political reality, and to be typically held by groups or communities. This first account might be used to explain the clearly extremist actions of certain devout religious zealots, whether Jewish settlers or Hamas militants. But it might also explain or provide the framework for innocuous or even happy events, such as religious celebrations or ceremonies.

The second (cynical) account dismisses such values altogether and proposes in their place a kind of Darwinian morality, viewing norms and values as outgrowths of the survival of the strongest and fittest. This "might is right" account—the same one presented to the Melos islanders by the Athenian generals in Thucydides' *History*—might be used to explain events which primarily reflect power struggles between groups or communities, such as the Phalange and the Palestinians in Lebanon, or Fatah and Hamas in Gaza and the West Bank, or Israel and the Palestinian people. Here the world is a jungle, and meta-biological entities simply fight for hegemony. They first articulate self-serving ends and then pursue them. A vivid example in our case is the building of settlements. In this account, the entity (here, the state) first identifies certain ends, such as building settlements. Then, after the fact, the entity develops the legal justification and or court rulings that reinforce those ends by entrenching them in public consciousness both as moral imperatives and as a natural state of affairs expressed by a set of codes and rules. For proponents of this account of the way moral values and legal norms have been formed throughout history, since it is power that speaks, it is no surprise at all that the "last word" on resolutions taken by the U.N. Security Council—with regard to Israel or to Iran, for example—is the United States veto.

The third (existentialist) account, while concurring with the second that moral values and legal norms are outgrowths of human history, views them as arising from the human face of that history. It is in accordance with this account that we may be reminded, as individual human beings, of who we really are, and manage to act as our individual selves, asserting our humanity. Whereas in the second account we are primarily driven by a cold-blooded, self-serving calculative sense, here that calculative sense is balanced by a more compassionate, other-caring sense. This account's distinguishing feature is its singling out of the individual as the main player in events—because it is as individuals, flesh-and-blood human beings rather than parts of a meta-biological entity, that we feel compassion or care or forgiveness toward others, and it is as individuals that we constantly grapple with moral choices, always feeling that there is some choice which is the right thing to do, and that it is for our self-betterment if we do it.

History's human face, then, makes an appearance when an individual, perhaps acting right up to that moment as a Phalangist in 1976 in the Tel Za'tar refugee camp in Lebanon, suddenly has his eyes opened and refrains from injuring or murdering another person for being Palestinian. Or when a would-be suicide bomber, acting right up to that moment as a zealot, suddenly realizes that the act he has vowed to commit in the heart of Tel Aviv will be a crime against humanity. In each of these cases, and also in less dramatic instances of compassion like those of Aziz Abu Sarah and Izzeldine Abuelaish, which we encountered in Chapter 2, individual human beings manage to throw off their mantle of xenophobic group identity and to instead assert the humanity within them. It has become commonplace to question, either out of the skeptical view that values are dictated by the powerful and victorious or in view of the increasingly visible variation of cultures around the world, whether we can speak at all about basic values that all human beings share. Do universal human values—does a universal human face—truly exist? Or should we instead expect (as well as respect, up to a point) totally different, and conflicting, values?

An unfortunate trend in contemporary political thought is to see the world not so much through the eyes of "human nature" (philosophy's traditional borderless scope) as through those of regions or civilizations or political systems or national or racial temperaments. From this borders-bound perspective, it is considered naive to search for a core set of human ends or values and more realistic to see the world as containing an assortment of different values and ends spread around the different political or civilizational cultures. Indeed, proponents of this view may even claim that recognition of and respect for this pluralism of human values is what defines a truly democratic and liberal perspective. In this world of variegated values, furthermore, where individual human beings disappear into or behind meta-biological entities such as states or political systems, the relationships that assume overriding importance are those between the meta-biological entities. For example, from the perspective of a "western liberal democracy" like the United States, Israel may appear to be a natural ally, while Iran or Hamas may seem a natural enemy—never mind the hybridity of the individuals who happen to be American or Israeli or Iranian or members of Hamas. Analysts may then draw various conclusions about how a particular state should handle its allies and its enemies, but the die of the distinction will already have been cast: that "east is east, and west is west, and ne'er the twain shall meet"—except when they clash!

This musing about universal human values may remind us of the question raised earlier about life and its worth: whether life's value is intrinsic or not. If it is intrinsic, our search for basic values can be cut short. If not, then we have to look elsewhere. But where then should we look? We can, making use of the three accounts described above, suggest that values can be considered either as existing prior to and independent of human history (for example, religious codes of behavior), or as being constructs or outgrowths of human agency. If the latter, then we can of course add that these values are merely consequences of the resolutions of power struggles in the world, the primary principle being "might is right," and so they shall remain. Or we can claim that they are, cumulatively, expressions of the compassionate rather than the hegemonic sense of human nature, but that they are constantly evolving, being drawn by ultimate principles which reasonable people would want to live by.

Of course one cannot deny the impact of the hunger for power—and the use of force and violence as its instruments—throughout human history. However, the fact that this hunger has been *a* salient feature of our history does not make it into an eternal law. I believe that the gradually increasing impact of a value-driven current in this history, rooted in the longings of individual human beings for a better world, has been and still is greatly underrated. Indeed, one can even argue that values and norms of human making, though initially informed by self-serving hunger for power as in the second account, slowly have become and are becoming more informed by compassion and the human face, as in the third account—almost the way the cave art of our early ancestors eventually bloomed as that of the Old Masters.

In any case, my own view is that while many values (such as best systems of government or codes of conduct) can indeed be culture- or time-specific, there *are* core human values, rooted in the compassionate impulse, which are on the whole independent of context, and which therefore are universally shared. By "universally shared" I mean that all the different values an individual identifies and aspires to as he faces moral choices in life—the values which tell him, in each situation, that a particular choice is the right thing to do and that he will be better for doing it—are ultimately guided by two main principles (about which I shall say more presently). I also believe we should not despair of the existence of these values, however ugly the world may sometimes seem. In a world that has come to be divided in accordance with a power scale between large meta-biological players, the only way we (all of us as human beings, not just those of us who belong to a bellicose state or a disenfranchised national group) can achieve a peaceful life and minimize conflict and violence is to continue believing in and to be guided by a value system or a moral order we, as human individuals, can all agree upon. If we take the individual rather than the state or some other meta-biological being as our starting point, and if we peel off enough of the layers we have inherited or constructed over our inner identities, we will indeed find that we share, impelled by our common sentiment for compassion, the will to do what we believe is right. Cumulatively, over time, those things which each of us considers "the right thing to do" converge as common values, coming to command universal consensus and to be considered almost self-evident moral truths.

The framework within which such a process can take place is the third account of human values described earlier, the account which features the human face and the compassionate or humane impulse in the motives of individual human beings, including their motives for establishing political structures for themselves. It is this account that allows for peacemakers to break meta-biological barriers: for Israelis and Palestinians to see each other as human beings, and to forge a common fight for the well-being of the two communities.

There remains the question of whether we human beings can agree on a list of these common human values.[3] As one way to identify the basic building blocks or what I called the main principles of such values, let us consider the following thought experiment: Suppose God tells humankind that he has decided to reshuffle the deck. In the changed world, people will not be reallocated the same qualities and resources they possess today—not even the language they now speak or the education or skills they now have. But before he shuffles, God tells us, he will allow us time to name a bare minimum of shared goods as "guarantees" that we can ask him for in the new state. There will be two voting rounds. In the first round, only one good will win: the one that gets the highest number of votes. In the second round, two or three goods can win. The winners will be the shared goods God will offer us in the new world. He allows us to deliberate freely among ourselves over this matter, and the voting is by secret ballot, as each of us can communicate our choices directly to him.

My contention is that, in such a situation, most of those deliberating in a reasoned manner will choose the same two goods: equality in the first round, and freedom (in both its positive sense, freedom *to do or be,* and its negative sense, freedom *from*) in the second. Equality will get the highest vote in the first round because the voters will want to make sure that they themselves do not miss out on whatever goods win in the second round. Once equality is assured, they will feel less edgy about which items will win the second round. One such item that can by reasoning be shown to be a basic concern to each and every person, is freedom, and I contend that freedom will be one of the winners of the second round.

Once these two basic goods, equality and freedom, are in place, it is possible, using them as building blocks, to construct—as in a game of Lego—an entire sphere of human values, with those toward the center of the sphere being more common to all human beings, and those nearer the surface being more context-specific. But this philosophical construction project is beyond the scope of this book; for our present purposes, identification of these two core values is enough.

To reiterate, I believe that there do exist core human values, rooted in the compassionate impulse, which are largely independent of context and thus are universally shared. As it turns out, the two identified in our thought experiment are converse sides of the same coin: freedom is the space necessary to enable human beings to develop in positive ways, and equality is the availability of that space for all.

The universality of these core values applies within societies as well as between them. Yet Palestinians living in Israel or under its occupation are denied both equality and freedom. And, though it may sound paradoxical, the Israelis are not free either: jailers and prisoners inhabit the same jail. The history of our region has bred intense anger and fear on both sides, and these powerful negative emotions strengthen the tendency of both (Jewish) Israelis and Palestinians to view members of the "opposing" group not as individual human beings with longings similar to their own, but rather as operatives of some larger entity, cogs in some meta-biological machine. If we wish to achieve peace and stability without oppression, it is vital that we focus on the human face—both our own and those of the "others"—and on the values shared by all.

5

What Does the Future Have in Store?

At the time of this writing, President Obama's special envoy for Middle East peace, Senator George Mitchell, backed by much of the international community and by parties to the conflict themselves, is quietly and methodically pursuing the implementation of a two-state agreement. After almost two decades of bumpy negotiations on an un-merry political go-round, many observers are understandably skeptical about his chances of success. But fifty or even forty years ago, anyone with a claim to expertise about Middle East politics would have viewed the possibility of a mission like Mitchell's as mere fantasy.

And yet, even back then, not everyone dismissed the notion. As many Palestinian Jerusalemites recall, soon after East Jerusalem fell to Israel's forces in June 1967, a friendly Israeli in a soldier's uniform went around knocking on the doors of well-known politicians and asking if they kept a Palestinian flag in the house. The soldier's name was Uri Avneri, and today he is renowned for his indefatigable activism in favor of a two-state solution, and for having been one of the earliest Israeli soldier-politicians (the other being the late General Matti Peled) to initiate dialogue with the Palestine Liberation Organization (the PLO).

Although already a project in Avneri's mind, the idea of establishing a Palestinian state in the territory that Israel had occupied in 1967 was not being entertained, especially as a *solution* to the Israeli-Palestinian conflict, by any nationalist political parties on the Arab side at that time.[1] Most of the politicians Avneri visited thought he was crazy. And when a few individual Palestinians living under occupation—particularly Hamdi Taji and Aziz Shehadeh (father of the novelist and human rights activist Raja Shehadeh) in Ramallah and Mohammad Abu Shilbayeh in Jerusalem—started touting the idea, it was viciously attacked, as were those who tried to propagate it. It took nearly three decades for this idea to become politically respectable, but today it is regarded as official policy by most countries in the region and elsewhere in the world.

In May 2007, almost forty years after he knocked on those doors, the same Uri Avneri participated in a debate with a newly controversial Israeli historian and author, Ilan Pappe. By that time the political scene had again changed: the two-state concept (as well as the once-ostracized PLO) had totally lost its revolutionary luster in left-wing circles. The debate, held in Tel Aviv by the Gush Shalom peace organization and attended by many veteran Israeli peace activists, was entitled "Two States or One?"

Avneri, still a zealous supporter of a two-state solution (as was Gush Shalom, which he founded in 1993), called upon the audience not to despair of his idea. Noting that he was eighty-three years old and had lived through the rise and fall of both Nazism and the Soviet Union, he pointed out that nobody had predicted the fall of the Berlin Wall before it actually fell. Theorists, he said, only scanned political surfaces; they did not have access to subterranean undercurrents that could suddenly surface in people's lives.

Ilan Pappe had been catapulted to fame in 2005 when, as a faculty member at the University of Haifa, he accepted an Arab student's Master's thesis on the forced eviction of Palestinians from their homes in the 1948 war. In the debate, Pappe insisted on one state as the only realistic solution to

the conflict. Israeli land confiscations and settlements, he said, had made the two-state option in-
feasible for the Palestinians under occupation; and
the option did not address the basic issue of the
right of return for Palestinians whose original
homes had been in what is now Israel itself. Pappe
reminded the audience of the meeting convened by
David Ben Gurion in 1948, in which the Zionist
leadership decided to expel a million Palestinians
from their homeland. The source of the Palestinian
tragedy, he asserted, was the concept of Israel as a
state that was both Jewish and democratic. As such,
Israel needed a Jewish majority, and its policies from
Ben Gurion's day to the present had been shaped by
that need. Zionism, he added, as it manifested itself
in the Middle East, had turned out to be a colonialist project predicated on land confiscation and ethnic cleansing. In his view, not only ought this historic injustice to be redressed; the very notion of a
Jewish democratic state is not viable, given demographic facts and trends such as rates of Arab population growth.

Pappe's point about the notion of a Jewish democratic state is at the center of a long-standing issue
in our region. Many Israeli Jews insist that Israel
can be both Jewish and democratic, meaning that it
can have a Jewish national character but still pro-

vide equal political rights for *all* its citizens. But many Israeli Arabs, both Muslims and Christians, argue that "Jewish democracy" can only mean "democracy *for the Jews only*." Clearly, a state with both Jewish and non-Jewish citizens is not democratic if it guarantees preferential treatment to one of those groups and disenfranchises the other.

The issue acquires an additional dimension when the territories occupied in 1967, with their largely Arab populations, are taken into account. Back in 1984, hoping to throw light on the implications of continued occupation, I called upon Israel to annex the occupied territories and extend citizenship to their Palestinian inhabitants; I also pointed out that doing so would risk, over time and through democratic processes, Israel's Jewish majority, its Jewish character, and even core symbols such as its flag. (After publishing a couple of articles along those lines I was invited to appear on television, where an interviewer asked me whether, if I became an Israeli citizen, I would be willing to participate in the army. Meaning to shock, I replied that if joining the army would enable me to walk around with an Uzi over my shoulder as Israelis did, I'd sign up any day.) My statements, which caused quite a stir, were intended to point out to the audience that Israel could not remain *Jewish* over time if it wished to retain a democratic system of government, nor could it remain *democratic* if it wished to retain Jewish domination over a disenfranchised and ever-growing Arab population.

The presence of large numbers of Arab residents in the occupied territories is often referred to as Israel's "demographic problem," but in fact the growth of the Arab population within Israel itself will eventually create the same "problem." Israeli Palestinians now number just over a million and make up about 20 percent of Israel's population. By some calculations, they will reach 50 percent through natural growth in the next twenty years. How, then, will Israel maintain its Jewish democracy? Sooner or later, as their numbers increase, Israel's Arab citizens will become the litmus test of whether a Jewish democratic state is, in reality and in the long run, indeed possible.

Apprehensive of this demographic trend, Avigdor Lieberman, formerly as a Knesset member and now as foreign minister, has proposed redrawing Israel's political map along demographic lines. Lieberman's basic position is that, in order to maintain Israel's Jewish as well as democratic character, it would make sense to strip Palestinian Israelis of their Israeli citizenship, disgorge from Israel the geographic areas where they are concentrated, at-

tach these areas to the West Bank, and finally annex
to Israel all the major Jewish population centers in
the West Bank which have been built since 1967.
(While Lieberman hasn't gone on record as saying that all Arabs living in Israel or the West Bank
should be expelled to neighboring Arab states, some
people suspect this is his real agenda.)

Both Pappe and Avneri reject Lieberman's proposal. In the debate Pappe drew upon the example
of the village of Baqah, East and West. Unlike the
more than five hundred Palestinian villages evacuated and totally destroyed by Israel in 1948, Baqah
was left largely unscathed, but like some other villages along the border, it was cut in two by the
Green Line established by the 1949 armistice. Half
of the town, Baqah West, came under Israeli rule,
while the other half, Baqah East, came under Jordanian rule. Baqah's small population, linked by
family and other fundamental ties, thus became
separated politically. While Baqah West is now an
integral part of Israel, Baqah East is now under Israel's occupation. Pappe pointed out that a mark of
Zionism's victory (even as noted in the Palestinian
press) is the refusal of the (Israeli Palestinian) inhabitants of Baqah West to be reunited with Baqah
East under the aegis of a Palestinian state. This is
what Zionism succeeded in doing, Pappe said: it

created distinct Palestinian identities, one that can only live in the independent Palestinian state advocated by Gush Shalom, while the other can only live in "democratic" Israel.

Pappe's general point was that Israel's "Jewish and democratic" character can only be achieved by means of ethnic cleansing or apartheid. He called for Zionism, as an ideology and as a structure, to be recognized as a colonialist movement, and to be replaced by a system of government that is truly democratic, allowing Palestinian residents full political rights and full participation.

Avneri, a self-professed Zionist but one who believes that, regardless of the past and of ideology, a two-state solution is both possible and necessary, put three questions to Pappe. Those questions, in my view, constitute the core of a well-intentioned rational discussion of the one-state and two-state solutions at this time. The first question was whether and how the truly democratic single state Pappe envisioned could come about. The second was whether such a state, if it did come about, would be *good:* that is, capable of providing decent living conditions for all its inhabitants. The third was whether such a state would be *just:* in other words, whether it was therefore *the* moral solution.

At the end of the debate Avneri claimed that his

questions had gone unanswered, and proceeded to answer them himself. Answering the first question, Avneri claimed that Pappe's single state would not come about peacefully, since the majority of Israelis would not vote for it; it could only come about through a war in which Israel was defeated. But such a war, besides meaning that the solution would be imposed by force rather than by consent, would entail an exorbitant human cost, putting the morality of this option in doubt. Addressing the second question, Avneri added that as matters now stand, even if the state were to come into existence peacefully, without war and without human suffering, it would necessarily be a state of unequal national partners, with Jews for a long time living the life of an exploiting class; thus it could not be described as *good.* Finally, as to whether such a state would be *the* moral or just solution, Avneri said that a seemingly moral solution that was perfect in theory but inapplicable in reality was in fact immoral, since in practice it would perpetuate the unjust status quo and would probably serve as a breeding ground for more extremism, such as support for ethnic cleansing. In effect, Avneri claimed that the perfect was the worst enemy of the good.

Pointedly, though, Avneri added that his difference with Pappe had to do with how far into the future they were looking: a twenty-year span versus a hundred-year span. In Avneri's view, a two-state solution that could be achieved in the present might end up creating the best conditions for future political fusion of the two states—first through economic cooperation and eventually through a European-style confederation or federation of states. To him, demanding an "unrealistic" and "costly" single democratic state was like insisting on tearing a slice from the future and trying to squeeze it into the present.

Although presented from the Israeli perspective, the debate between Avneri and Pappe defined in condensed and simple form the outlying boundaries of the moral landscape before us. Supposing that a democratic, multi-ethnic, multi-religious single state is ideal as well as inevitable, ought it to be forced into being, or must it be entered into through mutual consent? Viewed from the Palestinian perspective, would a two-state solution that by its very definition failed to re-create the pre-Israel past be unjust? One could also ask: Isn't the very pursuit of a goal that is in fact impossible—in this case, the re-creation of that past—itself unjust, if it prevents the pursuit of a workable solution? In any case, how would the establishment of a Palestinian state of the type Avneri advocates (an idea which may now be acceptable to the PLO leadership) address the concerns of Palestinians who would remain Israeli citizens but for whom the Zionist ideology is anathema, both in terms of its history and in terms of its instantiation in the state to which they belong and of which, ideally, they would be co-owners? Or the concerns of Palestinians in refugee camps who have been waiting for sixty years to return to their homes in what is now Israel, but who would not be able to fulfill that dream if such a so-called workable solution were indeed worked out? And for that matter, is an Avneri-type solution indeed possible or workable after all this time?

It is well at this point to consider what options we Palestinians, as a geopolitically disaggregated people, have before us, especially given the nature and weight of the international community's engagement in our affairs. Current political wisdom (the neutral international position) maintains that the way to solve the Palestinian problem is to break it down into manageable pieces: that rather than seeking a single solution that can apply to Palestinians everywhere, one should seek different solutions for the different Palestinian populations. The hope is that, taken together, these solutions will come close to a best option for the Palestinian people as a whole.

In this account, which corresponds both with Avneri's proposal and with my own, a two-state solution, preferably with those states delineated by the borders that existed before the 1967 June war, would constitute a cornerstone of a "best option" solution. A Palestinian state defined by those borders, with its capital in East Jerusalem, would accomplish a number of goals. It would:

end the occupation that began in 1967,

pacify the Arab world, which has made such a solution conditional to normalizing relations with Israel,

provide the Palestinian people with a home of their own,

allow Palestinians living in the diaspora who wish to return to their "homeland" or at least to acquire citizenship of the new state to do so,

free Palestinians living in Jordan who wish to do so to become fully Jordanian, create conditions for allowing Syria and Lebanon (mostly Lebanon) to reformulate their policies toward Palestinians residing in their countries,

allow Palestinians in Israel to feel more at ease with their citizenship-identity,

allow an agreed-upon number of Palestinians in the diaspora to be repatriated to Israel proper, and

allow for the initiation of a scheme of compensation for the Palestinian refugees.

Other benefits, too, would surely flow from the creation of an environment oriented toward peace rather than toward continuing conflict. A climate of peace in the Arab world would free minds and resources for addressing basic human needs: raising literacy rates, providing health services, creating new jobs for fast-expanding populations, bettering living standards, creating investment-friendly environments, and so on. For far too long the continuing state of war with Israel has been an easy excuse for straitjacketed economic growth and constraints on basic freedoms. Military failure has also been a direct cause of the rise of fanaticism at the expense of pluralism and tolerance.

Expressed in this way, however, this so-called political wisdom does not seem to have teeth, or teeth that are strong enough. Decades of negotiation and other measures have failed to bring about a two-state solution. Any number of reasons may be cited to explain this failure, from local resistance on both sides to the influence of powerful interest groups or governments which, for their own purposes, favor continued instability in the Middle East. Meanwhile, people in the region are encouraged to live in a two-state fantasy bubble, continuing to believe in what is marketed to us as the "peace process," even as the prospects for a two-state solution are fast dwindling before our eyes.

There are various possible outcomes of this situation. One is that the Palestinian Authority—especially now that it has accepted President Obama's call for "unconditional" direct negotiations—will agree to a less-than-optimum two-state solution: essentially a decapitated Palestinian state (that is, without East Jerusalem's Old City at its center) and one with a generally diminished and dismembered body; or, to change the metaphor, an archipelago state with no control over the "waters" dividing its component islands. Such an outcome can be brought about in stages by getting the two sides to agree on yet another transitional arrangement, without prejudice to either side's position regarding the final outcome. To help persuade the Palestinian side to accept this, the international community can make explicit its own vision of that final outcome. Thus Israel will be partially pacified by not having such a solution imposed upon it forthwith, while the Palestinians will be partially pacified by feeling that the international community will stand behind them when the time for a final decision arrives.

Failing the Palestinian Authority's cooperation in this process, another possibility is for the powers that be to begin reknitting a strategic relationship between the West Bank and Jordan, leaving Gaza (as well as Palestinians in Syria and Lebanon) for a later stage. A third possible outcome is that Israel, with or without international support, will maintain and beef up the existing system of governance in the West Bank for a specified period, pending further developments, while at the same time continuing the siege of Gaza. This third scenario might, at a later stage, feed into and merge with the first outcome or the second.

As matters stand, none of these three possible outcomes is likely to be received with enthusiasm by average Palestinians. (Hamas and diaspora PLO factions would certainly oppose any of the three developments, with more or less force depending upon how events unfolded.) In general terms, these outcomes are more likely to spark opposition and even serious resistance if they are presented (or are per-ceived) in the form of a "this is it" package. If so, instability will once again reign, and the "solution" will not have achieved its purpose (unless, of course, the unstated purpose is to maintain instability in the region). Certainly resistance will be greatly re-duced, at least temporarily, if initiatives are intro-duced gradually, in a kind of drip-irrigation method —as they seem to be being introduced at the mo-ment. On the other hand, it is not clear what im-mediate practical impact an American-sponsored two-phase negotiation process will have, or how av-erage Palestinians will therefore react to it.

To return to the "best option" two-state solution, it is clear that this would entail compromise, and therefore also opposition. Its proponents would need to persuade a sizeable portion of the pop-ulation to embrace it, creating support that would help contain the opposition and thereby foster longer-term stability. What I mean by containing opposition is, first, bringing the majority around to adopting the proposed solution and, second, mak-ing members of the minority feel they have a fair chance to be heard. The use of force or violence must be excluded from this process, recourse being made exclusively to public discourse and a demo-cratic method of decision making. This means that those in favor of this solution would have to "market" it to those opposed to it, as well as to the so-called silent majority.

The major emotion-laden point of contention would be the issue of Palestinian refugees' right of return. But the discussion, though needing to take account of the deep emotions involved, can only be resolved rationally, and I have already suggested that it should have the theoretical form of being between *right* and *good*. In straightforward terms, the best-option scenario addresses the public good in a way that relegates what many Palestinians consider their right of return to a secondary place. Although deemphasizing this right would anger many displaced Palestinians, the argument in its favor is quite persuasive, both politically and morally. The argument involves weighing the rights of individuals against the well-being of the Palestinian people as a whole. Placing the refugees' right to return to their original homes at the top of the priority list would prevent the establishment of the best-option scenario (which is by definition a *negotiated* and therefore *conditioned* two-state solution), and thus would prevent even a partial, watered-down version of that right from being implemented. Even if the totality of individual rights were to be weighed against the public good in this way, those rights would remain secondary. To argue otherwise would be to deny the existence of this particular public, the Palestinian people, as a political unit with its own identity.

If that meta-biological being, the Palestinian people, did not exist as a single unit on the world political stage, individual rights could readily become key elements in the formula. But one cannot both have one's cake and eat it, as the saying goes. Where the pursuit of individual rights is clearly an obstacle to the realization of the public good, and where, also, the public in question is made up of the very individuals who are claiming those rights—under such circumstances, the rational conclusion is that it is *better* for those rights to be forfeited. Cases like this, in which the rights of individuals are pitted against the good of the group to which they belong, are not the only instances in which good and right may be mutually exclusive: even for individuals themselves, the exercise of their rights may not always be for their own good, as in the case of smoking. Nor need rights be forfeited only in favor of the good: it may be necessary to forfeit one right in order to implement another. For example, supporters of a Palestinian state might forfeit the right to build up an army to gain the right to build up an economy.

In the process of public discourse on this matter, certain refugee populations, unwilling to forfeit the right of return, might choose to be discounted, that is, neither to have their rights pressed for nor to have them resolved. Thus, they might ask to be left out of any deal between representatives of the Palestinian people and Israel. Even that could probably be part of the settlement: a mechanism allowing refugee populations to choose among various options (repatriation to the Palestinian state, compensation, continued residence in host countries with or without new citizenship in those countries, and so on) or to postpone their decision until a later stage. Or they might simply refuse to participate in any way; this choice could simply be a personal expression of political conviction without any formal political implications.

Ideally, President Obama will put the so-called best-option solution on the table for the leaders on both sides to take back to their communities for public debate and, on the Palestinian side, new elections. In this way, the solution will have the best chances for public endorsement and therefore longevity.

But let us assume that nothing of the sort happens, and that instead of taking clear and direct steps toward such a solution we find ourselves facing the prospect of another forty years of in-between existence, neither independent in our own optimum state nor enjoying normal political rights in the state which rules us. Under such circumstances, what other future paths might we follow? Commenting from a completely academic perspective (that is, a perspective divorced from any real power-brokering capability), many Palestinians, in different forms and for different reasons, now express a preference for a one-state solution: a single state in which Palestinians and Israelis would be equal citizens. Some have proposed this scenario as a negotiating tactic, others as an ideal solution, yet others as a fallback position. Strictly speaking, of course, this type of solution does not seem to be right around the next corner either.

Other models have been tentatively suggested, including federal as well as confederal systems linking cities, regions, or states together. One possible path that, I believe, deserves serious consideration by both Palestinians and Israelis (and also by the international community, which might present it as a challenge to an unyielding Israel) is for Israel to offer Palestinians in the West Bank and Gaza full civil and human rights so long as a permanent settlement has not yet been reached. The result would be an interim step: a single-state but electorally non-

democratic consensual arrangement, that is, a mutually agreed-upon conferral by Israel of a form of
"second-class citizenship" on all Palestinians currently under occupation who wish to accept it. For
those Palestinians, this result would be like having a
state in the weak sense defined in Chapter 3—belonging to the state without being its co-owners—
even while continuing to feel they owned the *country.*

The advantage of this scenario (primarily, but
perhaps not only, under the in-between living conditions already referred to) would be to create a possible point of intersection which could be agreed
upon by the two sides, and which, at least as a transitional stage, would maintain Jewish *ownership of
the state* while guaranteeing Palestinians their human rights and all services a state normally provides
for its citizens, including their collective cultural
rights. From the Israeli Jewish (and especially the
right-wing) perspective, this model holds several
attractions. The state (Eretz Yisrael) would extend itself—under certain provisos, to be stated—
throughout the coveted "Judea and Samaria" region,
in parallel with the extension of Palestinian access
to all areas within Israel. Jews would be able to settle
anywhere in that extended domain, except on oth-

ers' private property, as long as they did not limit or harm Arabs' rural and agricultural development there. The Arabs absorbed into Israel by such an annexation of the currently occupied territories would not acquire votes in the Knesset, and thus would not threaten to transform the state from within. And Jewish citizens would retain exclusive control over the military and other important state functions. The only negative side, for Jews who see matters that way, would be having to put up with the Arab population living among them.

From the Palestinian perspective, this scenario would be a far more bitter pill to swallow. It would require them to give up the dream of having a Palestinian state, and those now living under occupation, as well as those in the diaspora who decided to participate in this experiment, would have to make do, psychologically, with being subjects rather than citizens in their own country. So, you may wonder, what could Palestinians possibly find attractive in such a model? Several quite hefty benefits may be listed.

Diaspora Palestinians afflicted by insufferable feelings of exclusion from their homeland would at last be able to make the longed-for journey back to it, either to visit or to settle down—since civil rights surely include the right to return to one's homeland.

A system of material compensation for Palestinian refugees and others whose properties were confiscated could be implemented forthwith, alleviating hardships and creating new opportunities.

Palestinians living in this expanded Israel would be able to exercise basic human rights, including the rights to travel freely within the state, to work wherever they could find a job, to rent and buy property and to live where they chose, and to access state services such as health, education, social welfare, retirement benefits, union rights, financial assistance schemes, security protection, and the legal system. In sum, they would enjoy all rights except voting and being voted for in elections to the Knesset and holding elected office.

Simply put, in this scenario the Jews could run the country while the Arabs could at last enjoy living in it.

In his debate with Pappe, Avneri suggested that adopting his two-state solution might be a more conducive step toward a single non-Zionist state than calling for one immediately. In the absence of an Avneri-type two-state solution, the "second-class citizenship" model proposed above might be an even more conducive step toward that outcome— and far more so than a present or future make-believe Palestinian state. One advantage it would have as a transitional phase is that it could come about either through agreement or, failing that, through a unilateral move by Israel to (partially) correct the blatant affront to human values of the current state of affairs. The right-wing politician Moshe Arens, as mentioned earlier, has proposed extending full citizenship to Palestinians in the West Bank. For Israeli Jews, the downside of this proposal is the perceived threat to the state's Jewish character. For Palestinians, one drawback is the exclusion of Gaza's population from this offer. But Arens's suggestion at least tries to address a Zionist-expansionist point of view while taking into account the need to rectify an abnormal and inhumane situation—and in doing so recognizes this abnormality for what it is rather than dismissing it as merely a passing phase of so-called occupation.

The arrangement I have described skirts around the concerns raised by Arens's idea: Israel's Jewishness (at least in the short or medium term) and the

severance of one part of Palestine's Arab population from the other. It is worth noting that this type
of arrangement, in which people voluntarily partake
of civil but not political rights, is not altogether
strange to our region: Arab Jerusalemites have lived
in this kind of situation for the past forty years, and
Palestinian Israelis who support the Islamic movement do not, on principle, participate in the political system. So if, as we look toward the future, neither a one-state scenario with equal rights for all
citizens nor a "best option" two-state scenario is a
realistic possibility; and if, instead, we seem to be
moving toward either a less-than-best two-state
scenario (if a settlement is reached at all) or a one-
state scenario of binational apartheid (if no settlement is reached)—then the arrangement I have
outlined may well serve all parties concerned better
than any other. In any case if the United States, for
whatever excuse given by Israel, cannot bring Israel
to end the occupation, or to stop building settlements or carving up the Palestinian countryside for
its ever-expanding infrastructure, the least it might
do is to challenge Israel to grant the occupied Palestinians full civil rights for as long as it keeps unilaterally disposing of their lands. (As noted in the In-
troduction, this arrangement may be self-annulling;
that is, one of its positive consequences may be to

make people on both sides take the best-option two-state solution, and the compromises that go along with it, more seriously than they have thus far.

What the future holds remains, of course, an open question. But its openness has less to do with our not knowing what will happen than with our not knowing, or not quite thinking through, what we really *want* to happen, and therefore not working to bring it about. The major question in the background is what a Palestinian state is worth, meaning both what the state would really be *for*—what needs it would satisfy—and what would be a fair compromise to make, or even a fair price to pay, to bring it about. This is not only a question for Palestinians to ponder. It is for Israeli Jews to ponder as well, both in terms of how it relates to what they want a Jewish state for, and in terms of what compromises, territorial or ideological, they may need to make as the issue of a Palestinian state is being considered.

6

Who Runs the World, "Us" or Thugs?

We have already encountered one indefatigable Israeli peace activist, Uri Avneri. Abie Nathan, who passed away in Tel Aviv in 2008, was another. Back in 1978, when Shimon Peres was busily supporting the establishment of settlements in the West Bank, Nathan was the first Jewish Israeli to go on a hunger strike in protest. (In retrospect, given what we now know about the settlements' role in sabotaging progress toward a two-state solution, Nathan might have been a far worthier recipient of the Nobel Peace Prize than Peres.) And Nathan did much more than protest against settlements. He founded an offshore Voice of Peace radio station, with John Lennon's help. He volunteered his time and effort around the world, wherever natural or man-made disasters struck. In 1966, a year before the June war, he even flew a civilian aircraft from Israel into the enemy territory of Egypt, defying the laws of both countries and risking his life. Upon landing in Port Said, he requested an audience with Egypt's president, Gamal Abdel Nasser, to hand him a personal plea for peace. In 1991, after repeatedly disobeying an Israeli ruling outlawing meetings with PLO officials, and after publicly meeting with Yasser Arafat, Nathan spent six months in prison.

Abie Nathan was, in short, a striking example of the human face in the Israeli-Palestinian conflict. And, given our tendency to identify people by set meta-biological definitions, including definitions like "Iranian" and "Israeli," which now seem to be set at opposite poles, his history merits close attention. He was born in Iran to a Jewish family, spent his adolescence in India, was a pilot in the British Royal Air Force during World War II, volunteered his flying skills to Israel in the 1948 war, and then settled in Israel. In more ways than one, Nathan exemplifies the hybrid individual whose humanity defies our rigid meta-biological categories.

But, a skeptical reader might retort, however celebrated for their commitment to peace people like Nathan and Avneri may be, and however guided by universal human values, surely their impact on the conflict in our region pales beside that of tank drivers, gun-toting militants, and hard-core party apparatchiks. The *real* world, this reader might argue, is designed and run by power-grabbing realists, not by ineffectual idealists or daydreamers. On this view, the trajectory of political history is determined primarily by a selfish human nature which relies on the use of force and equates might with right, and Abie Nathan stands out precisely because he is a bright exception to this depressing rule.

If we accept this version of reality, my comments at the end of Chapter 4 about the existence of shared values which could inform our political endeavors seem almost irrelevant; the moral political project described there is of very limited value if most people instinctively incline toward acts inspired by the darker side of human nature. But instead of readily accepting this version, we can challenge it by trying to determine how rare or exceptional the Abie Nathans of the world really are. This will require us to consider, however sketchily, the question of whether people's actions are primarily selfish. It will also require us to revisit the question of whether history is primarily shaped by force. The stalemate between Israelis and Palestinians is an appropriate example to use in our challenge, because it is cited by both sides of the argument: both those who argue that only force works and those who argue that force not only fails to work but is actually counterproductive.

Let us begin with a question about human actions: What causes us to (choose to) act in one way rather than in another? Classically (to put it somewhat simplistically), two general domains have been suggested as possibly holding answers to this question: base instinct or emotion, and the rational or calculative faculty. The image of a spirited horse running wild in open fields is often invoked to illustrate the first of these domains, and the image of a horse that has been tamed, bridled, and controlled by its master to illustrate the second. The ancient Greeks drew a similar line between *phusis,* the ugly side of human nature, and *nomos,* the laws that reasoning human beings devise to keep their own impulsive natures in check. Thucydides, describing a rebellion which took place on the island of Corcyra during the Peloponnesian War, explained that such disorder sets in when the law collapses, allowing human nature to rear its ugly head. According to this picture, human beings are primarily impelled to act by their base passions; but having discovered,

through their reasoning faculty, the drawbacks negative effects of living in such a state of nature, they
eventually establish an orderly system of interaction
for themselves and mold their actions to fit that system. Typically, in this model, egotism is associated
with our baser nature and considered primary, while
altruism is associated with our civil state and considered secondary.

Although this model seems overly simplistic, it
has strongly influenced our understanding of political affairs. It is generally assumed, for example, that
unless a proper balance of power is maintained to
keep the world players in check, the players will run
loose, pursuing their own selfish interests, and international order may collapse. Witness, in this regard, the concern of some nuclear powers that other
nations they do not consider "mature" enough may
also acquire nuclear capability. On this view, too,
individuals are *primed* to act in their own selfish interests, heedless of others; their primary imperative
is affirming a space for themselves. Only secondarily do they come to allow others space, and this
only when, using their rational calculative faculty,
they determine that allowing others such space is a
better guarantee for maintaining or expanding their

own space. That is why this model assumes that egotism is primary while altruism is secondary.

Those who view the world from this perspective, then, are bound to conclude that Israelis (and people more generally, including Palestinians) are typically greedy and selfish, and that Abie Nathan is an oddity. Likewise, when we hear about Izzeldine Abuelaish's reaction after losing his three daughters in Israeli rocket attacks—that Israelis and Palestinians must teach each other love and respect, and that he could never hate a human being—we are likely to dismiss Abuelaish as yet another exception that proves the rule. Indeed, many observers assume that Israelis and Palestinians harbor such strong and entrenched feelings of hatred and vengeance against each other that, if peace were ever to be realized, they would have to be dragged to it in chains! In other words, those who view the world from this perspective assume that we are primed to see each other and the world in a negative light, and therefore they portray the peacemakers among us as oddities.

We cannot, of course, disregard the beastliness with which human beings often treat one another, for example the way Palestinians in Gaza acted against each other as the Hamas militia engaged in a violent takeover of power. Nor can we disregard, again in the Palestinian context, the sheer selfishness of many officials, who seem to see being part of a fledgling national authority as a chance to become wealthy or powerful rather than as an opportunity to build up a polity wherein all citizens can be assured of all their rights. Nevertheless, we do not have to hold the cynical (so-called realist) view of the world described in the previous paragraph. There is a second model that is equally compelling, if not more so. To contrast the models, let us again consider the two domains posited as sources of motivation: base instinct or emotion and the calculative or rational faculty. According to the first model, human behavior, including mental behavior or processes, is prompted by *either* one *or* the other of these two sources: a person is impelled to act, or to formulate or recognize connections in thought, either through an emotional mechanism or through a calculative mechanism. And, typically, the act is consecutively composed, being first rooted in the emotional and egotistic (self-conscious) domain, and only later tempered by the cognitive (other-conscious) domain. Thus, it is claimed, the primary motivations for action are egotistic, and only secondarily are our egotistic motivations tempered by our calculative (or rational) faculty. We can call this model of the sources of human behavior *disjunctive.*

The second model, in contrast, proposes that emotion and cognition are not primarily separated, and that the "ugly" side of human nature is not the exclusive property of the former. According to this unified or *conjunctive* account of human behavior, a typical mental or physical action is simultaneously informed by a mixture of cognitive and emotional factors. Natural instinct is not monopolized by the emotional or egotistic disposition, nor is the cognitive faculty innocent of that disposition: instinctually, we can be as caring, compassionate, and loving toward others as we are prejudiced in favor of ourselves; and calculatively, we can be as brutal to others as we are accommodating to them for our personal gain.

There is room in both these accounts to explain acts that are purely emotional or passionate—for example, motivated entirely by feelings of hatred or revenge or fear for oneself, or by feelings of love or care or compassion or fear for the other. But whereas the disjunctive model posits the typical act as being composed of two consecutive tiers, the conjunctive or unified model posits it as being composed from the two domains simultaneously. One implication of this unified view is that we need no longer see the world from a cynical perspective. That is, we need not see ordinary human acts as primarily selfish or threatening, requiring a staying force to keep them in check. And we need not see behavior such as that of Abie Nathan as inexplicable. Rather, we can view it as exceptional in the context in which it occurred but as eminently explicable. Furthermore, we need not consider norms and values to be "add-ons," designed at a later stage of human evolution to curb our base natures. Rather, we can see them as outgrowths of both our natural dispositions and our deliberations. Nor should we assume that it is better for reason to be sovereign in our dealings with one another, for our reason, according to this model, can be just as "inhumane" as our baser instinct.

Again, this unified model does not exclude cases in which actions may be purely informed by passion or emotion. But there is no reason to consider actions motivated by passions such as fear or anger to be the rule, and those motivated by care or compassion to be the exceptions. Indeed, whenever only one genre of motivation is involved in an action we could view that as an exception, regardless of which type of emotion it expresses.

A unified theory of human behavior, then, provides *one* account of human motivation. It views the primary impulses for action not disjunctively but rather conjunctively, without any assumed severance between emotion and reason or between types of emotion such as egotism and altruism. On this view, we all consider our own actions to be morally driven; that is we all generally tend to act as we think we should (Palestinians, for example, by resisting Israel, and Israelis by trying to suppress Palestinian resistance). People on each side believe their own actions are morally right but the other side's actions are beyond the moral pale. Thus if we accept this unified view, we are still faced with the problem of how to go about reconciling two conflicting morally driven perspectives (a problem we shall return to later on).

The use of the word "side" in this context reflects the category jumps—from individuals to meta-biological entities and back again—that we make in thinking about ourselves and others. Israelis slip into seeing Palestinians (and Palestinians slip into seeing Israelis) as instances of a "side" which acts immorally, and they are therefore surprised when some event forces them, contrary to their internalized meta-biological view of the world, to recognize the real-life human being in front of them, a person like themselves. Typically, they conclude that what they are seeing is an oddity: that most Palestinians (or Israelis) are not like the one whose humanity they have just recognized.

On this cynical view, peace movements and peacemakers are at best celebrated but secretly pitied. They are seen as counting as but a drop in the ocean, and political advisers do not encourage leaders to take them seriously. But I hope it is clear by now that this so-called realist view of human behavior is not necessarily a *realistic* view. It can be argued—and there is much polling evidence to support the argument—that human dispositions to act are far more favorable to a state of peace than they are to a state of war. On this more optimistic view, the sentiment for peace among Israelis and Palestinians may be preeminent, and peacemakers like Abie Nathan and Izzeldine Abuelaish are visible indications of a solid underlying reality rather than oddities.

Our skeptical reader may object that while a unified account makes sense in theory, in fact human beings (and states) do not seem to behave in accordance with that account, but rather seem to act primarily out of self-interest, and to use force to pursue that interest. Even if this reader accepts the claim that a universal moral language is indeed possible and is not inconsistent with human nature, she may still argue that, in world history as it has actually unfolded, the dominant influence has been the "dark side" of human nature. We just need to look at the Israeli-Palestinian conflict, she may say, to remind ourselves of this sad fact.

Gandhi, responding to this claim in *Hind Swaraj*, pointed out that in human dealings with one another, as evidenced throughout history, acts of goodwill infinitely outnumber those dictated by selfish greed and hate, which pit individuals and nations against one another in bloody conflict. We might add that the cynical appraisal of the world is often based on dramatic events and on short periods in the life of nations, and is thus incomplete. It is true that outbursts of violence have occurred and continue to occur in the lives of both individuals and nations. Human beings or nations, at certain periods in their evolutionary histories, can and do resort to force to achieve their perceived interests, as is evident from even a cursory look at the list of invasions of one country by another over the centuries. But the questions we are pondering here are whether history's unfolding pattern so far has shown moral and political evolution or its opposite, and whether, given human nature, what we consider to be our human values can only be secured by a militarized infrastructure or a balance of fear and force. We could answer these questions in the Gandhian spirit, by arguing that these violent, base-natured outbursts in the lives of nations are simply "interruptions," and will eventually be smoothed over by a reorientation of human behavior in accordance with the unified or conjunctive theory. More often than not, when children who are prone to be aggressive grow older and become more familiar with their calculative skills and their contextual human surroundings, they fairly quickly learn to temper that aggressive egotistic instinct with their calculative skill, which makes them rework the nature of their relationships with others. More typically, as I have already argued, they may, through increased contact with other human beings, become aware of an intrinsic sympathy or instinctive compassion they feel toward others—the sentiment that eventually becomes the psychological underpinning of our moral sense.

Even states brought into being by acts of force

tend, over time, to adjust that force by a tempered view of their place among nations. Basic moral values such as freedom and equality, first slowly molded to become (in democratic systems of government) the associative cornerstone of their own citizenry, eventually come to be considered the only acceptable cornerstone of international association as well. Often, indeed, the citizens of such states are quicker to reach that recognition than their respective governments. Where this is the case, history shows that those governments come under pressure from their own citizenry, pressure that results either in changes in foreign policy or in a change of government. It would not be natural, for instance, for an enlightened public in a true democracy to tolerate its government's friendly relations with a fascist regime bent on aggression and violations of human rights. Indeed, western democracies are prominent examples of histories in which bloody ontogenesis eventually gave way to legal and moral normative systems which, as I have argued, reflect an inbuilt human nature already disposed toward the development of such systems.

The science writer John Horgan notes that in recent years revisionist biologists and anthropologists have challenged the classical claim of humanity's warlike nature. Horgan refers to a growing scientific literature which traces a "positive" (that is, decreasingly violent) historical trajectory in human affairs, indicating that human violence is more context-related than biologically inherent, and therefore that it is also tamable. He quotes the psychologist Steven Pinker as observing that studies show that war is not inevitable, though neither is peace.[1]

The realist*ic* view, then, is one that accounts for the effect on the world of what I have argued is the gradually and historically transformative character of human behavior. Given human beings' capacity to act either way—either selfishly or altruistically—this can only be explained by the exercise of conscious human *will,* which constantly reaches out (in existentialist fashion) for an ever better and more refined moral existence. I suggest that the better existence sought is defined by the core human values identified earlier: freedom and equality. If we postulate a gradual historical convergence toward those values, as well as a gradual refinement and universalization of their application, we may then regard the evolution of law and of the practices of political systems, not as necessarily reinforcing those systems, but as seeking to emancipate them from their historical foundations in force and self-interest. This emancipation is dialectically connected with the emancipation of individuals themselves and their increasing participation in the political system, or their transformation from object (passive) to subject (active) or from subject (passive) to citizen (active). Such transformative processes in one political system tend to trigger parallel processes in others, and tend eventually to affect the way one system allows itself to treat another.

We could view these historical processes as a general pattern, rather than as descriptions which are true of specific instances of political orders. To deny the existence of this process of evolution in the identities of individuals and political systems is to be blind, for example, to the ways in which the concept of "citizen" has evolved since Athenian or Roman times, or to the way attitudes toward slavery or toward women have changed—or indeed, even to the way marriage as a relationship between two individuals has developed. On the other hand, to recognize these transformational processes is to recognize identities, whether of individuals or of political systems, not as temporally or qualitatively static—frozen in slices of time—but as constantly being shaped by an internal emancipatory agency or will.

We will soon see how this understanding of the nature of identity bears on negotiations, and therefore
on the making of history. History, on this view,
evolves along a moral trajectory, however painfully
slow its evolution may seem (to the point, sometimes, of creating the illusion that history cyclically
repeats itself), a trajectory that reflects the active
agency of the human will.

Here our skeptical reader may speak up again. Even,
she may argue, if we believe that political realities
initially created by force eventually yield to a humane order, and also that a better means than force
can always be found to achieve positive political
ends, we still have no answer to the burning question before us: Why have the Israelis and the Palestinians, unable so far to resolve their conflict by
force, also been unable to resolve it by resorting to
reason? In particular, if we also believe that even
when people's motives are selfish they eventually
use their reasoning skills in deciding how to act,
why hasn't the application of pure reason, by showing the two sides where their interests converge,
magically resolved the conflict? Indeed, negotiation
based on reason, is what most observers consider to

be the only way out of the present impasse. But just as force (as I have argued) is neither necessary nor capable of bringing about positive political ends—and in the history of this conflict has in fact been counterproductive, entrenching hard-line positions on either side—so reason, as exemplified by negotiation, not only is insufficient for achieving such ends, but often has calamitous consequences.

We can demonstrate that reason is not sufficient by simply reminding ourselves of two points. First, reason typically informs us not *what* to think but *how to act on* what we think, and thus, in human relations, there is no rational best-case solution of the kind we expect to find in mathematics. Second, even if such a rational best-case solution existed, there is no guarantee at all (as Aristotle taught us) that we would choose to pursue it.

Regarding the first point, it is patently clear that neither Israelis nor Palestinians ask reason to tell them what to think. Rather, what they think—each side's respective moral outlook—is already in place before they consult reason. For example, if Palestinians think that Israel should not exist as a state, or that Israelis should live in constant fear, they can apply reason to devise "best-case" methods to oppose that existence or to create that fear. Or if Israelis think that Palestinians have no legitimate claim in Palestine and should lower their expectations of a negotiated deal, they can use reason to find "best-case" ways to minimize Palestinians' benefits from such a deal. The decision of what to think is made first; the execution thereafter can be as cold-blooded and vicious as they come. This is why the consequences of resorting to so-called reason can be calamitous.

It is important to recall here that I have already argued against the "disjunctive" theory, according to which human beings are primarily disposed to act selfishly rather than altruistically and their actions are typically motivated by only one of the two sides of human nature (either passion or reason, but not both). Instead, as I argued, human beings in general, and Israelis and Palestinians in equal measure, act as they think they ought: that is, in accordance with their moral values. This should immediately tell us that neither side's position is defined by "base instinct" that may later be tempered by rational calculation: rather, both sides' positions are shaped by moral outlooks informed by their respective self-definitions. Therefore, the solution to the puzzle before us does not lie in getting one side or the other to recalculate how best to achieve their selfish interests; instead, it lies in getting the two sides to see eye to eye on the moral values involved, and in so doing, to somehow redefine themselves.

In order to understand why reason is insufficient, and why the moral outlooks or values guiding each side in the negotiation have to be considered an integral part of that negotiation, let us return to the first point mentioned above: that, in human (rather than numerical) relations, there is never one rational optimum or best choice in any case. To believe there exists only one course of action that is "the rational thing to do" is to believe that reason tells us *what* to think (what to decide to do), not just *how* to think (how to go about deciding what to do, or how to go about finding best ways to implement what one has decided to do). But it is quite evident that this is not the case. Examples occur every day in which two parties, informed by conflicting interests, employ their respective reasonings to achieve exactly contrary objectives. Here someone who believes that negotiations proceed mechanistically, according to prescribed rules, might retort that when parties disagree, as they do in the Israeli-Palestinian conflict, reason dictates that they converge on identifying a common objective and then determining the steps needed to achieve it. Furthermore, that person might add, when two parties, by resorting to reason, do manage to find a common objective, they tend to choose it rather than stick to their original positions. According to this line of thinking, then, reason tells us both that it is up to the parties to identify such a common objective—which itself implies that such an objective *exists*—and that, once they identify it, they will choose it over their original positions.

In line with this view of reasoning, scholars of negotiation theory, game theory, and now artificial intelligence have focused on developing models of a paradigmatic negotiation that follows prescribed mechanistic rules. However, it is not clear that such modeling covers all possible cases, and in particular the Israeli-Palestinian case may disprove the principles on which such modeling rests. Evidence of this may be gleaned from any number of events, but let us consider the latest efforts personally sponsored by an American president. Invited to Camp David by President Bill Clinton back in 2000, Yasser Arafat and Ehud Barak reportedly clashed over the issue of the Noble Sanctuary in Jerusalem (the Dome of the Rock area for the Muslims, and the Temple Mount area for the Jews). Was it to be under Muslim (Palestinian) sovereignty, or was it to have a horizontally two-tiered divided sovereignty? Clinton's formula (a two-tiered approach), which cut through the stated positions of both sides, presumably aimed to identify a possible common objective or point of intersection between the Jewish concern for history and the Muslim concern for existing reality. Nonetheless the clash occurred, and all three leaders left Camp David feeling outraged: Barak and Clinton at Arafat's intransigence, and Arafat at Clinton's offer, which to him seemed deeply derogatory. Are we to conclude that Clinton's proposal, while informed by a rationally correct reconciliation principle (that is, a dictate of reason), was not properly prepared or presented? Or should we conclude that it failed because of irrational (that is, unjustifiable) intransigence by one side or the other? Observers tend to oscillate between these two explanations, either faulting the negotiating setup or blaming one of the two sides—not surprisingly, the Palestinian side—for irrational intransigence.

More generally, observers are often struck by what seems to them a perennially irrational attitude on the part of one or both sides. Israelis are fond of quoting a famous quip by the late Abba Eban: "Palestinians never lose an opportunity to lose an opportunity." Palestinians have long protested that in negotiations with Israelis they are expected to accept less than their full due. Israelis have claimed in response that "the Palestinian people" never existed in the first place as a full-fledged legal owner of the country, and that *they* are expected to give up a tangible good (territory) in exchange for nothing more than the Palestinians' verbal promise that such a territorial settlement will indeed bring peace. Observers, meanwhile, have questioned whether there has ever been a potential common objective between Israelis and Palestinians, and if so, whether they have simply failed to identify it or whether, in spite of its obviousness, one or both sides have rejected it out of intransigence.

Perhaps these observers are right to suspect that such a rational common objective has never existed. To assume that a common objective exists is to assume that reason defines conclusions or end points instead of paths or routes by which to reach predefined goals. But consider situations—and the conflict we are dealing with is sadly a paradigm of such situations—in which one or both sides view life itself as expendable. To recall our earlier discussion, people see life as expendable when they deem some value so essential that without it life ceases to be worth living. When such a value is on the line, negotiations, however rationally pursued, are futile. At the Camp David meetings in 2000, the value in question from Arafat's standpoint was Jerusalem, or its place in the collective Muslim, and therefore political, psyche. With regard to that value, Clinton's proposal did not fit into political coordinates Arafat could accept. (He may have later paid with his life for that position.) In the classical example, recounted in Thucydides' Melian dialogue, the value for which the Melians were prepared to give their lives was freedom. The German philosopher Immanuel Kant famously argued that everything in life was exchangeable except dignity, whose underpinning was what he called "autonomy of the will." So, whether the cherished value which is felt to be threatened is a core religious symbol, or a value such as freedom, or a human condition such as dignity, in such situations a non-zero-sum negotiation model that relies on the identification of a common objective is quite likely to fail. Where life is deemed worthless in the absence of dignity or honor or freedom, what can there be to negotiate about?

For those of us who seek to transcend the present Israeli-Palestinian stalemate, it is vital to understand the limits of reason in negotiation, and hence

what else, other than raw reason, we should be looking at. Imagine a typical negotiation setting in
which two parties with fixed identities or attitudinal dispositions face each other across a two-
dimensional plane surface which defines their eval-
uations of potential exchanges of a certain range of
goods. We can call this common surface a rational
space. This space maps out the different possible
combinations of dispositions by the two parties to
make exchanges among the range of goods, with
those dispositions represented by lines originating
where the parties themselves are positioned in the
space. Now imagine that the parties wish to negotiate over one particular good (such as a piece of
property, which one side might buy or exchange for
another item). In theory there may be a number of
possible points of intersection of the two sides' attitudinal dispositions, of which one intersection point
may indeed be an optimum exchange option for
both. This point, fitting the "dictate of reason" paradigm, will both exist and be identifiable.

But what if we imagine another geometric shape
for our negotiation setting, admitting two rational
spaces instead of one, thus making the shape three-
dimensional? As an example, again consider the

Melian dialogue. Imagine the entirely different moral outlooks of the two negotiating parties as lying on separate plane surfaces: the Athenians looked upon the Melians' freedom as a good to be exchanged for something they assumed would be unexchangeable for the Melians (their lives), while the Melians looked upon their lives as expendable for something they viewed as truly unexchangeable (their freedom). In this situation, no intersection point between the parties could possibly exist, as they functioned in totally separate rational spaces informed by their different moral outlooks. More generally, according to this model, in some cases two parties to a negotiation do not have the same range of potentially exchangeable goods spread before them, simply because their moral values are irreconcilably different. (The existence of two irreconcilable ways of thinking rationally can also explain cases where one or both sides seem to choose not to do what they know is in their own best interests—a situation that Aristotle called *akrasia*, or weakness of the will.)

In the meantime, it is important to emphasize the inescapably sealed nature of the two-planed rational space of this second model. Simply, however the negotiations are carried out, the two sides will never be able to reach agreement if the primary aim of one side is to dispossess the other of a good which the other considers unexchangeable on pain of death (or, less dramatically, of termination of the negotiations). This two-planed rational space, then, rather than irrationality, may explain a particular stalemate or deadlock, say over Israeli settlements or Palestinian refugees' right of return. There is a corollary to this: if and when the sides thereafter reach an agreement, this necessarily implies that the parameters have fundamentally changed, turning the negotiation setting into a single plane. To use geometry again, whenever an intersection point is posited between the two sides, that point must necessarily lie on a (new) single plane on which the two parties are positioned. This significantly implies a convergence of moral outlooks, that is, a fundamental change in the self-definition or identity of one or both parties to the negotiation.

Perhaps a good example of this is the way the Israeli government and the PLO came to view each other: at first, neither side's self-definition allowed it even to contemplate sitting down with the other, and each side, guided by its own values, searched for ways to achieve peace almost by discounting the existence of the other side. Years of second-level diplomacy failed to bring the two sides together. The turning point came only when they stopped regarding refusal to sit down with the enemy as part of their self-definition—who they were and what they stood for—and instead decided it was an exchangeable commodity that they could give up for the chance of peace. In the first phase, we might say, the sides were positioned in separate rational spaces or surfaces, and in the second phase (through a transformation of aspects of their self-definition or identity) they came to be positioned on the same surface, where substantive negotiations could begin. What had been two negotiation surfaces—two distinct and separate rational spaces defined by separate moral outlooks—became a single surface when those moral outlooks converged.

I am not arguing that only the second model can explain deadlocks in negotiations, but rather that some issues cannot be dealt with in accordance with the first model, and that negotiators must therefore take care lest pushing an issue too far turn the tables upside down, as happened at Camp David. And I am pointing out that when two parties disagree over an issue, there is not always a common objective for both which is definable by reason.

A related misunderstanding is to assume, when one party or the other does not seem to be acting rationally, that this is due to weakness of the will *(akrasia)*, which prevents it from doing what it knows is in its best interest. Scholarly debates about akrasia have generally assumed the existence of *one* range of rational courses to take (in our geometric language, one rational space). The underlying assumption is the existence of one unique object of knowledge (knowledge of which course is the rational one) which the people involved can acquire, and the question is how to account for those who know what is rational for them to do and yet choose not to do it. But just as in a negotiation between two parties, there may well exist not one but *two* ranges of seemingly rational courses that a side might take, each informed by a different value (moral outlook), and these may appear to have no intersection or common point. Akrasia may well be an expression of this kind of indeterminacy: the existence of two seemingly irreconcilable ranges of rational choices and ends. Acting upon one such choice, the akratic person may be viewed as having acted upon a preference for one of the two values. (This case differs from that in which the person fails to do what he believes or knows to be the *one* thing that is best for him to do.)

While my claim that the predominant feature of our composite human nature is positive may be a welcome and refreshing thought, holding out hope, my other arguments in this chapter—that neither by force nor by reason alone can Israelis and Palestinians chart a better future for themselves—may seem quite depressing. But my next point may again offer hope. In pointing out the need, when confronted with stalled negotiations, to go "outside the box" of reason and think about who the protagonists are—how they define themselves, and how to bring about a convergence of their moral outlooks so that negotiations can proceed toward a happy conclusion—I have not yet mentioned one important feature. This feature is often overlooked, and more often simply forgotten, in contemporary political discourse, but I believe it is a crucial agent in the transformation of protagonists' self-definitions, and one that can make it possible to "clinch" an agreement where one seemed elusive before. This feature is *faith*.

It can be argued that faith, rather than force or reason, has been the determining force of political history. This is clearly the case when one considers major religious events and movements, and it may equally be the case for secular events and situations. Not only religious faith, but also what we may call secular faith—faith in ourselves as human beings, faith in what changes we, as individuals and as groups, can bring about or create, faith *that* we can bring about such changes—may well be the missing piece of the puzzle, explaining what impels us, in the end, to exercise our will by acting in one way rather than another. (How we do this is a topic for the next chapter.) If, as suggested earlier, reason does not define our goals but only shows us how to bring them about, then perhaps we need to have faith in our ability to bring about a particular end, or to reach a particular goal, if we are to make that goal a reality.

Faith, in other words, as a belief or confidence in oneself and in what one sets as a goal for oneself, can *determine* what otherwise (if we relied on reason alone) would be an *indeterminable* point of agreement and one that might also elude us. Commenting on the failure of the 2000 Camp David talks, an Israeli diplomat surprisingly pointed the finger at neither Arafat nor Barak, but at Clinton himself—primarily for lacking the strength of conviction required at the crucial time to push an agreement through. One type of faith, then, is the strong belief which a key player in a negotiation must have that, if he takes the risk and makes the final move to clinch an agreement, he will succeed. According to the Israeli diplomat, Clinton seemed to lack the conviction that, if he put some pressure on, he would receive support from the American Jewish community (as, the diplomat added, he would have). Likewise, it may be argued that President Obama can succeed in bringing about peace in the region only if he makes a similar leap of faith: determining what otherwise would be an indeterminable point of agreement, and marshalling support to win the parties over to it.

But what exactly do I mean by an indeterminable point of agreement? Simply, it is any theoretically possible agreement, regardless of whether it later comes to be realized. Back in 1967, when Uri Avneri knocked on doors looking for a Palestinian flag, an agreement on a two-state solution was such a point, as it still is today. The point is indeterminable because we cannot tell in advance whether the agreement will be realized or not. When dealing with human decisions, we cannot "forecast" the outcome like tomorrow's weather. To call the point *determinable* would be to claim we could predict in advance, as with the weather, that it would most likely, or all things being equal, or "with a 70 percent chance," later be agreed upon. We would understand, of course, if the future didn't quite turn out as predicted—whether that meant rain on our picnic or failure to reach a two-state agreement—because we realize that we do not actually "know" the future, and that unforeseen developments may make our forecasts inaccurate. An *indeterminable* point, in contrast, is one about whose prospects we are not in a position to foretell anything. Its chances of occurring are just as good as its chances of not occurring.

But I am making a further suggestion: namely, that since in general we can't tell whether any specific point we might pick out (such as a two-state agreement) is determinable in the sense described or not, it must therefore be indeterminable. If we claimed, after a particular agreement had in fact been realized, that the point of agreement was therefore determinable all along, our claim would be based on a logical error. The error is the classical existential one of supposing that it is possible to deduce a particular premise (identify a specific agree-

ment) from a universal one (a list of several supposedly possible agreements). If I claim to identify,
from a range of possible solutions, a particular solution and then claim that solution to be determinable, my claims are based on the erroneous logical
step of existentially instantiating from a universal
premise. The famous Harvard logician W. V. O.
Quine, in explaining this point, alerted us to the
distinction between going lion hunting and going
hunting for a particular lion. In retrospect, after
catching one, I clearly couldn't claim that I had been
hunting for *this* specific lion. Similarly, it is wrong
to assume, before it has been actualized, that a particular point determinable by reason in fact exists.
Recalling our geometry, if by a determinable point
we mean one which lies on the same plane or rational space as the negotiators, we will simply be unable to identify it, because all theoretically possible points will be indeterminable, lying in abeyance,
so to speak, or suspended between two rational
spaces, "waiting" to become a point on one of them,
and possibly never getting that chance at all. (The
Camp David negotiation illustrates the latter type
of point, as does Thucydides' Melian dialogue.)

Translated to the world of action, what this indeterminacy means is that solutions are *made*, not

discovered. This is why in human relations, unlike mathematics, we need *faith* in what we set out to do, and why it is faith, rather than rational calculation, that allows us to make agreements, as well as to keep them once made. Of course, someone could claim (reverting to our earlier discussion) that the fact that solutions are made rather than discovered is precisely why *force* is needed to establish and maintain political solutions, and that, indeed, sufficient force unilaterally applied can determine what is otherwise indeterminable. This might seem like an argument in favor of unilateralism. Some might argue that Jews in particular, given their history, have no choice but to pursue this line of logic: to rely on their own might, however detrimental its use may be to others, as a way to ensure their security, or at least to minimize their vulnerability as much as possible.

But is this "line of logic" valid? Looking at Israel's history reveals two seemingly contradictory features, which we encountered earlier in this book: its almost always successful, unilaterally implemented military moves, side by side with the political consequences of those moves, which seem to require even more unilateral military moves. With each "successful" military incursion into Lebanon over the past few decades, for example, Israel has only sown the seeds of yet another incursion, with the military risk factor becoming higher each time. Reflecting on this pattern, one Israeli security expert made a penetrating comment: that although Israel has been winning all its military battles, it has all along been engaged in the wrong war. What he meant by the wrong war was Israel's quest to "settle its place" among the countries of the Middle East or to "normalize" its existence, goals he believed could be achieved only through a political settlement, not through the use of force. However, unlike military decisions, which one party can take unilaterally, a political settlement requires engaging the second party. This is where negotiations (in the very general sense) come in. And this is where raw reason, as we saw, does not necessarily work, and where we are now considering whether faith is needed.

Generally, when we hear the word "faith," we think of religion and God, but faith plays an equally powerful role in our secular lives. Whether it is faith in God or in ourselves, faith has the power to "move mountains" when nothing else can. Secular faith, as I am calling it to distinguish it from its religious cousin, involves or draws upon several features, including *vision* and *will*.

Before turning to these features, we should consider the way faith runs counter to a malignant disease which is prevalent in our region, namely *mistrust*. Among Israeli Jews, for example, it is primarily mistrust in the willingness of a Palestinian partner to commit to a genuine peace agreement, and mistrust in the life-or-death reliability of an international ally which might play the role of guarantor to such an agreement, that makes Israel hesitant to throw caution to the winds. Mistrust, or lack of sufficient trust, is why both the failed Oslo peace plan and the also failed Road Map for Peace included steps conceived as "confidence-building measures" —tangible and independently verifiable moves that, when implemented by one side, should have encouraged the other to take further steps toward a full agreement. Famously, however, the confidence-building phase of the process produced the opposite of its intended effect, destroying whatever mutual confidence had existed at the beginning of the process. The supposed confidence-building phase, in other words, was instead a breeding (or confirmation) ground for mistrust. Thus, while the disease afflicting the two sides and preventing them from reaching agreement—lack of trust or confidence— was correctly diagnosed, either the wrong medicament was prescribed or its dosage was miscalculated.

Sometimes identifying a specific measure in advance as a necessary confidence-building measure can be a complete mistake. Shortly after President Obama took office in January 2009, he sent former senator George Mitchell to our region to attempt to restart negotiations. Mitchell soon declared that negotiations could not begin until Israel ceased the expansion of settlements; he had Palestinian President Mahmoud Abbas repeat the same mantra. But almost immediately both leaders had to back away from that position, as it quickly became obvious that the Israeli side was not willing to engage in negotiations on that basis.

Senator Mitchell correctly identified settlements as pivotal, from the Palestinian perspective, for a two-state peace agreement: negotiating toward the establishment of a Palestinian state would seem an exercise in self-delusion if in the meantime Israel continued to chip away at that state's projected territory. Thus Mitchell pointed his finger at exactly the issue that is the source of Palestinian mistrust in negotiations. A total freeze on settlement expansion, including in East Jerusalem, would indeed have inspired confidence among Palestinians that

Israel might be seriously willing to negotiate the kind of two-state solution that Palestinians could accept. Since Israel, however, evidently wished to keep settlements as a negotiating card—most likely with the intention of giving up only the absolute minimum of them during negotiations and not relinquishing those in and around East Jerusalem—Mitchell was unable to get the commitment from the Israeli prime minister which he sought in order to dispel Palestinian mistrust.

But if Palestinians' mistrust has to do with Israeli designs on the territory of a possible Palestinian state, Israelis' mistrust may be more fundamental, seemingly being rooted in fear for their *lives*. This fear (typically discussed in terms of "security concerns"), is so deeply embedded in the psyche of Israeli Jews, and has been so incredibly exorcized from that of the Palestinians, that it is almost impossible for either side to understand its workings on the other. Palestinians cannot believe that Israelis live in perpetual fear (for their lives), and Israelis cannot understand how Palestinians live without such fear. (I am not here just referring to individuals who are readily prepared to sacrifice their lives for their cause, or individuals who have become so frustrated with their living conditions that to them life seems almost worthless. Among Palestinians there may well be a more fundamental underlying cultural or religious disposition to believe in the reality of death so strongly as to view life as being on a par with death, or even of far less value.)

Given the political interplay between what is expressed in the highfalutin language of "security concerns" and the more down-to-earth fear that is palpable in Israeli society, it is clear that those negotiating this issue need to view Israel's entire population, rather than simply the few individuals sitting around a conference table, as the real protagonists in the negotiation. An analogous argument can be made on the Palestinian side, with regard to an issue such as the deep psychological craving for "return." This point reminds us of the earlier emphasis on the need to widen our scopes as we try to identify who the real protagonists are in a negotiation. Negotiators admittedly always have to work within political parameters set by their leaders, and more generally—especially in democracies—by their respective populations. But in our region the two populations, Israeli and Palestinian, play particularly large roles. In identifying them as the *real* parties to the negotiations, I mean that we (as analysts or observers trying to understand the situation) should regard the negotiation as taking place in the homes, streets, and meeting places that make up the real world of people's lives, rather than behind the closed doors of a conference room.

With this in mind, we can begin to discern how to treat the disease we have already diagnosed, and to see why our previously prescribed medicaments have not worked. Mistrust, or lack of trust, is not simply a theoretical concept which can be addressed mechanically by experts at the negotiating table; it is a vibrant public emotion. In the confines of the conference room, the issue of security, for example, can be dealt with in technical terms by the experts. But this issue, which concerns the real fears of real people, must also—and sometimes primarily—be dealt with at the emotional level, and at that level every member of one public or the other becomes a party to the negotiation. If the official Palestinian negotiator agrees, as a trust-building measure, to proscribe firing at Israeli settlers but one or more Palestinians nonetheless fire at settlers, clearly it will be hard to convince the settlers that Palestinians can be trusted. Likewise, if the Israeli government agrees to proscribe settlement expansion but some such expansion nonetheless continues, it will be hard to convince Palestinians that the Israeli government can be trusted. And indeed, in one form or another, this has been the exact experience of Israelis and Palestinians since the signing of the Oslo agreement in 1993.

Perhaps a better way to deal with the problem of mistrust would be to go back to the drawing board and start over, redefining the protagonists, the space of the negotiation process, and the issues to be addressed to cure or alleviate the disease. With regard to the protagonists, we should look beyond the individuals who attend negotiating sessions and focus instead on the population conglomerates or national groups on both sides of the political divide. These meta-biological entities are the ones that must be won over, and the way to win them over is to awaken their component individuals to the need and the opportunity to take charge and to draw a new path for their lives. Similarly, to define the space of the negotiation process, we should look beyond the walls of the conference room and focus on the entire political reality lived by Palestinians and Israelis. In other words, we should discard the notion that negotiations take place among a few carefully selected people meeting behind closed doors; in its place, we should recognize that in fact real negotiations are being conducted constantly by all of us, in our homes and in the streets. And finally, in defining the issues to be addressed, again we should transcend the normal list of items typically bickered about by negotiators (settlements, roadblocks, walls, number of guns, media incitement, schoolbooks, and so on) and focus instead on a holistic vision of a projected future in which all these disparate issues will seem insignificant, having melted into a much larger and far more appealing picture of peace, progress, and safety for all.

The comparison between this secular vision and the religious paradigm (projecting the City of God on earth) should not be underemphasized: what we need to do is to redraw the current reality so as to provide, to both Palestinian and Israeli publics, an alternative vision of the future so overwhelming that it will make present-day political squabbling pale in significance. As noted earlier, faith, vision, and will are all indispensable to our quest for a better future. It should now be clear why the first two are necessary: we need vision to "see" and then to project that earthly heaven, and we need faith to believe it is within our capacity to bring the earthly heaven into existence. As for will, which is discussed in the next chapter, we need it to infuse the protagonists with the new faith.

Shifting our focus to the future is a way to transcend the present mistrust of each side for the other and thereby to transform that negativity into a positive vision of an imagined new world where such mistrust does not exist. Such a course of action is not totally foreign to political leaders. Shimon Peres has been known to market the "New Middle East" —a peaceful and economically vibrant geographic space where Arab and Jewish skills, contacts, and resources combine to bring untold prosperity to all. Such visions can encourage the skeptical, the fearful, and the lethargic to take on the risk of peace. Leaders are important in articulating the visions, but even Moses needed Aaron as interlocutor: the vision has to reach the masses on both sides, not simply the wealthy or the elite. To make this happen, the leaders need to possess the qualities of a prophet whom people can trust and in whom they can come to believe. That is, the leaders need to have a vision, to have faith in that vision, and to be able to rally the people to share that faith. The vision of the peaceful and prosperous future may take any of several forms: one state, two states, confederation, federation involving one country, or two, or three, and so on. But whatever form it takes, it has to be a moral political order, and its foundation must be the two elements of freedom and equality.

7

How Can We Move the World?

Archimedes, it is said, claimed that if he had a long enough lever, he could cause the world itself to move. If, as I have argued, a moral order purged of reliance on force is indeed feasible; and if, too, history's political trajectory confirms that human beings are naturally more disposed to act humanely than otherwise; and if, most important, we have *faith* in such a humane future, then we may ask ourselves if we can devise a moral Archimedean lever with which to facilitate the world's movement toward that future. As an expression of the human will, this lever would, by conscious choice, replace force as a means of political transformation. When applied appropriately in a political conflict, it would reinforce the emancipatory transformation referred to in Chapter 6 and hasten the formation of the world's moral order. To borrow an expression from Gandhi, the lever would be like the force of love or of the soul. And to borrow a metaphor from another field, applying the moral lever rather than resorting to violent force would be like adopting a therapeutic rather than a surgical approach to the enhancement of human health.

Political practitioners, unfortunately, often prefer surgeries to therapies, believing the use of force to be the most effective shortcut to solving problems. And indeed, surgery sometimes seems to be the only available solution. But in the short term, violence often produces the opposite of its intended effect—as it did when the Arab states went to war against Israel in 1948 and ended up losing, not only the territory already allocated to Israel by the United Nations, but also half the territory allocated to an Arab Palestinian state. And in the longer term, what at first seems like a solution may turn out not to be one at all. Worldwide examples abound of militaristic aggressions or policies that initially seem successful but, in the end, fail in their objectives or even rebound against the countries that initiated them. Consider Israel itself, which, although created to provide a safe haven for Jews, has arguably placed them in greater jeopardy than ever before: in deadly conflict with both their neighbors and the population they evicted to establish that supposed haven. Furthermore, it can be argued that the more force Israel uses to counter this threat, the more threatened it becomes. Israel is believed to have nuclear weapons of its own, and certainly it has access to them through powerful allies;[1] but one or more of its potential enemies may acquire them in the foreseeable future (such as Iran) or may already possess them (such as Pakistan). It is true that Israel disabled Iraq from developing such a weapon, and it is said to have prevented Syria from even beginning to build one, but 100 percent vigilance is impossible, and the human risk involved is far too high at even half a percent less than one hundred. Any nuclear stand-off between Israel and such enemy states (or advanced militant groups with access to tactical nuclear weapons) could only be temporary, and would surely end, in a tragic lose-lose situation, with devastation on both sides, including the near-total obliteration of the largest Jewish population that has ever congregated in one geographic area. And, needless to say, the military danger exists even in the absence of nuclear weapons. The fact that Israel's "waist" is only nine miles wide—often cited to support its territorial expansion into West Bank territory, or its need to ensure military supremacy over its neighbors, or both—becomes less and less relevant given the external danger of constantly advancing long-range weapons delivery systems and the internal challenge of a fast-increasing and adversarial Arab population under its rule.

Indeed, as already mentioned in this book, it is a striking fact that the more Israel has, through the use of force, succeeded in planting itself in the territories it occupied in 1967, the more in jeopardy it has placed its project of establishing a democratic Jewish state. Even its military victory in 1967 backfired against this overall project: the Palestinians, a people it had set out in 1948 to delete from the map as a national entity, and whose parts in Egypt's Gaza, Jordan's West Bank, and Israel had been severed from one another for two decades, were, to all intents and purposes, reunited, now under Israel's aegis, but constituting a radical threat to its exclusively Jewish character.

But Palestinians and other Arabs, even those who agree with what I have just said, may not draw the appropriate conclusion as they consider their own options. The question confronting them harks back once again to the claim about the role of force in history: Even though Israel deprived them, unjustly and by force, of the basic human values of freedom and equality, is their only choice to use violence themselves? Or would they, by resorting to violence, be simply digging themselves into a dead end of history rather than making use of history's moral lever? In Gandhi's book *Hind Swaraj,* written as a dialogue between characters identified as Editor (who speaks for Gandhi) and Reader, the Reader voices the so-called realist's view which we came across in Chapter 6: the claim that nations and history itself are forged by violence. There is no other way to make India free, he declares, than by using violent force. Gandhi's response is stunningly powerful: wars and violence, he says, are but aberrations of the flow of human history. They do not constitute it, as is often claimed. On the contrary, history is "a record of every interruption of the even working of the force of love or of the soul."[2] If it were otherwise, we human beings would have depleted ourselves by now, and "not a man would be found alive today." Consider, Gandhi adds, the survival of the family as an institution in spite of the millions of quarrels and dissensions among relatives, and you discover the preeminent power of the force of love or of the soul.

In Gandhi's view, using violence to rid India of British occupation would merely replace one type of occupation, one type of ethnic or racial rule, by another. Garibaldi's recourse to armed force in Italy, Gandhi argues, unlike Mazzini's dream for that country, left it in the same state of occupation it had experienced under Austrian rule. Likewise, the way for India to become free and exercise real self-determination or home rule is through *swaraj*, the inner freedom and self-sovereignty individuals achieve by remaining true to their humanity, rather than through adopting Britain's system of values (including, above all, its "value" that the use of force can be morally justified). Given that means and ends are inextricably intertwined, the use of violence, if successful, would only replace British rulers by Indian rulers—it would not make India free. In a free India, the British would live side by side with the Indians, but under a totally different system of values.

Gandhi's reflections on India are well worth transposing to our context: "My patriotism does not teach me that I am to allow people to be crushed under the heel of Indian princes if only the English retire. If I have the power, I should resist the tyranny of Indian princes just as much as that of the

English. By patriotism I mean the welfare of the whole people, and if I could secure it at the hands of the English, I should bow down my head to them. If any Englishman dedicated his life to securing the freedom of India, resisting tyranny and serving the land, I should welcome that Englishman as an Indian."[3]

Gandhi here clearly refers to India and its civilization not as race or religion but primarily as a system of moral values or a humane order. Patriotism is not racial chauvinism or self-love and self-adulation, but "the welfare of the whole people." Thus if Palestinians were to take their cue from Gandhi, they would cease looking upon their own patriotism as a religious or national cul-de-sac, and begin viewing it instead as an overarching affinity with the land and its multifaceted racial as well as religious history. They would have to transform their vision of a free Palestine from that of a princedom to be ruled by Arab Palestinian "princes" to that of a land of a free people living by moral values. In such a land, an Israeli could be just as patriotic a Palestinian as could an Arab Palestinian! Indeed, to adopt such a perspective on patriotism is to see the political landscape in a radically new light. The chasm in that landscape suddenly is no longer between "us" and "them"; rather, it is between "us" in the currently prevailing system of values and "us" in a new one. More particularly, in this light, a philosophy of renouncing the use of force means more than simply resorting to nonviolent action: more significantly, it means renouncing our underlying assumptions of what the conflict is about, and replacing them with new assumptions which will henceforth guide our pursuit of a moral order.

Acting as an Archimedean moral lever in history or as a Gandhian power of the soul thus involves far more than simply using nonviolent means to achieve moral political ends. Some proponents of Gandhian nonviolence overlook this, seeing nonviolence as a weapon which can be used by *us* to *force them* into submission. But in thinking this they are simply importing into their argument in favor of nonviolence the entire theoretical paraphernalia of more typical conflicts in which the use of force is paramount. In classical conflicts the parties are typically posited as one another's enemies, and the guiding imperative is for one party to subdue the other and subject it to its dictates. Extrapolating from this paradigm, some assume that the purpose of nonviolent action, too, must be to pressure the other party and force it into submission. However, a key feature of the Archimedean moral lever, and of Gandhi's power of the soul, is *transformation*, not subjection. The guiding imperative here should not be winning over the other side, but winning the other side over—not making the others act against their will, but changing their will, making it congruent with your own.

As we saw, Gandhi's *Hind Swaraj* has a humane rather than a chauvinistic objective. But in some struggles for national liberation, proactive nonviolence may have, and may need to have, a "repellant" effect instead of (or in addition to) a "gravitational pull" effect—for example, when its goal is to persuade the other protagonists to keep their distance or to withdraw. The Palestinian intifada of 1988 arguably had the dynamics to produce both effects, namely to bring about an end to the Israeli occupation and the establishment of an independent Palestinian state. In that first intifada, what began as (and to some extent remained) a low-level violent stirring of the population against the occupation became, largely through organization by the local leadership, a comprehensive strategy of civil disobedience. Many segments of the civilian population under occupation—workers, officials, students, shopkeepers, middle-class professionals, and so on—participated in a nonviolent program consisting of two parts. The first part, under the general slogan of "freedom *from*," involved severing themselves from the occupying power's instruments of control (trade, government functions, the labor force, and so on); the second, under the general slogan of "independence," was to construct their own instruments of self-rule, building their state from the bottom up. Civil disobedience transformed the occupation from a low-cost, high-benefit enterprise for Israel into a burdensome and costly project. Skilled and unskilled workers stayed away from Israeli worksites. Consumers boycotted Israeli goods. Palestinians flouted civilian orders (such as building and zoning permits and licensing procedures), ignored military instructions (such as summonses), obstructed routes used by settlers, and stopped paying taxes. Tax officials, policemen, and others employed by the military administration tendered their resignations and thus ceased to serve as buffers between the army and the civilian population. Confronted with this conscious withdrawal of Palestinians from the system, Israel called on its army to reestablish its hegemony over the population. But as armed units stormed villages, civilian men and women of all ages resisted with barricades, fists, and rocks (people had not altogether banished physical force from their arsenal of responses, though it was not their primary "weapon" of choice). Peaceful mass protests spread like wildfire: marches, strikes, town meetings, underground political leaflets. National slogans appeared on walls, national flags on electric lines. In addition to all of these activities to "push away" the occupation or "disentangle" themselves from it, and as the complementary side of the civil disobedience campaign, Palestinians formed far-reaching institution-building and self-help task forces or committees which operated in all areas of services required by the population, including health (doctors and nurses), education (school and university teaching), food security (home-based farming), and even legal committees to resolve disputes, to give some examples. And, last but not least, the people engaged with both the Israeli and foreign media to communicate their moral message and thereby to chip away at Israel's image both at home and abroad.

The first intifada's strategy of proactive nonviolence was expressed in its two main slogans of *freedom* and *independence.* Freedom meant disengagement from Israel's occupying tentacles or structures, and independence meant the replacement of those

structures by autonomous ones in all areas of civilian life. The vision was that such a strategy, through
a nonviolent process of fact creation on the ground,
would eventually *persuade*—rather than *force*—the
Israeli public and the Israeli leadership to believe
that a negotiated settlement, based on a two-state
solution, was in their best interest.

Nonviolent forms of national struggle have
proved successful in various cases around the world,
but in the Palestinian case the intifada did not have
the desired effect. Instead it created a paradoxical
situation. Although it made Israel fully cognizant of
the cost and burden of the occupation, and although
it drew the international community into a more
active role in the political process through which
Palestinians hoped to achieve freedom and independence in their own state alongside Israel, yet
the overall political result was a purgatorial reality, in which the Palestinians could neither reach
that sought-after independence nor fully integrate
themselves into Israel. In other words, they were
neither free from Israel nor equals within it.

Is it still possible for the Palestinians to find a
way out of this dead end, and to achieve their "independence," by once again practicing nonviolence?
They certainly cannot do so by replicating the 1988

strategy of civil disobedience, since the first intifada's whole philosophy was based on the reality of
the submergence of Palestinian life in Israel's economic and political system. The frame within which
this reality was maintained was the rule of force,
and yet the internal structure of the occupation (the
administration, the economy, and so on) paradoxically depended upon the Palestinians' acquies-
cence—however unwilling—to that reality. Therefore they were able to disrupt the reality by acts
of disobedience (of two types, disengagement and
the establishment of self-rule structures). Since the
signing of Oslo, in contrast, the occupying power
has withdrawn from Palestinian civil life and relocated itself to the population centers' outer limits.
In Gaza, it relocated to the entire district's outer
limits. There it "took off its civilian dress" and re-
claimed its real form as an army. Palestinians in Ramallah could no longer stage a disobedience campaign by, for example, refusing to pay taxes, or
resigning from official posts, or refusing to obey
summonses or building permits. They could, as an
act of protest, demonstrate—but when Palestinian
demonstrators marched through the streets of Ramallah in 2000, during the protests that launched
the second intifada, they could not stage sit-ins at

Israeli offices, military or civilian, because such offices were no longer there; nor did they face Israeli
soldiers on the streets, because the Israeli military
had pulled out. The only remaining points of encounter between the two sides were at the outer
boundaries of the city, where the marchers, once
they arrived, could do little but either turn back
or provoke a confrontation; the young participants
chose to do the latter by throwing rocks at the soldiers guarding the roadblocks to the city. Eventually, after a run of similar confrontations, with the
soldiers responding to the hand-thrown rocks by
shooting gas canisters, then rubber bullets, then real
bullets, young Palestinian demonstrators began to
fall down like birds from the sky. Their deaths
sparked the population's anger against the Palestinian Authority, whose armed security personnel were
criticized for not returning the Israeli fire or doing
anything else to protect the protesters' lives. Thus
was unleashed a bloody cascade of violence which
swept Israeli-Palestinian relations into a totally new
orbit.

The 2000 intifada made it clear that the 1988
strategy could not—because of the changes since
the signing of the Oslo accords, according to which
local self-government replaced government by the

occupying force—be replicated. More recently, since the Israeli decision to build the separation wall/fence to encircle Palestinian areas, various civilian protests have been held to stop construction of the wall or to change its path, some with limited success. Some Palestinians have argued in favor of widening this wave of nonviolent protests, and perhaps turning it into a general strategy to end the occupation. However, it is not clear how this could be accomplished. Even if the protests were coupled with selected forms of passive resistance, such as boycotting Israeli goods manufactured in settlements or encouraging an international boycott of everything Israeli, the hoped-for result could only be the creation of enough international pressure on Israel to *force* it to capitulate. Once again, therefore, and contrary to the philosophy of the 1988 intifada, all the features of a classical conflict situation would be recreated, with Israel viewed as the enemy to be defeated, and with nonviolence seen merely as an alternative way to exert pressure.

It is of course possible that, in the long run, international pressure on Israel will yield results, as it did in South Africa. It is also possible that such pressure will be supported by dissident Jewish voices from within Israel. For example, in 2010 the former

Knesset speaker Avraham Burg (son of the founder of Israel's National Religious Party, author of *Defeating Hitler,* and, famously in recent years, Zionism's doomsayer) joined street protests in the Sheikh Jarrah neighborhood of East Jerusalem against takeovers of Palestinian-inhabited houses by Jewish claimants. But it is far from certain, given the way Israeli settlements have tampered with political geography, that such pursuits can lead to the kind of separation from Israel which would be acceptable to the Palestinian side. In fact it is likely, given Jewish history, that international pressure, instead of causing Israel to break asunder, will have the opposite effect, making it coalesce to become as hard as solid rock.

Creating pressure was arguably also the strategy of the 1988 intifada. Even so, the purpose of that pressure was not to *defeat* Israel, but rather to win it over to a Palestinian vision of peace. Many of the leaflets produced by the intifada leaders were written in Hebrew and were specifically addressed to the Israeli public, which was viewed as a potential partner for peace. If, in today's changed circumstances, a two-state solution is no longer within reach, it may be more important than ever to think of ways to apply the Archimedean moral lever, but with a clear vision of the moral order we wish to achieve. The political context in which such a lever needs to be applied seems to be an increasing entanglement of the two protagonists, or an unfolding reality of a binational Israel that practices apartheid. Here again, the way to construct such a lever is to identify and carry out actions which will change the will of the people on the other side, and will do so by *winning them over*. In other words, this Archimedean moral lever would function in precisely the same way as Gandhi's conceived power of the soul, namely, as a *pull* tactic—or as a means of making Israelis Palestinian, while guaranteeing that identity to be a moral one rather than racial or religious.

Pressure aimed at defeating the other side is quite different from pressure aimed at "winning hearts and minds." Resorting to the former generally means assuming that the other side's identity (as well as its position) is fixed. In contrast, exerting pressure with a view to creating a gravitational pull presupposes the ability to transform that identity (and position) in positive ways. To put it another way, wielding the moral lever would involve considering the surrounding political circumstances from "outside the box." From inside the box, the protagonists are typically assumed to have fixed identities (and positions), and the question raised is whether it is best for one party to employ violent or nonviolent forms of pressure as a means of defeating the other party or forcing it to concede a desired objective. From outside the box, protagonists' identities need not be regarded as fixed or pre-set, and the question to be raised is whether (and what) actions by one party will alter or shape the other's identity in ways that will make it possible to reach that desired objective. (These observations relate as much to negotiations between the two sides as to the general political vicissitudes of their conflict.)

We can reduce the main features of an Archimedean moral lever (and of the outside-the-box approach) to two main elements, both of which ultimately rest on what we singled out in the last chapter as the determining human disposition that overrides both reason and force—namely, faith in human beings as makers of their own destinies. The first element is agency, or will, as a means of altering one's own identity or another's; it draws on the notion that human identities are not pre-set or static but are constantly being shaped or formed by conscious acts of will. The second element is the notion of the de-ideologized human being or citizen—admittedly a clumsy expression, but one which I hope conveys the idea; it draws on the notion that ideologies are merely second- or third-order constructs relative to basic (first-order) human concerns.

As examples of the first element, consider two cases from the Israeli-Palestinian context: the electoral defeat of Israel's Labor Party in the aftermath of the 2000 Camp David talks, which resulted in the replacement of Ehud Barak by Ariel Sharon as prime minister and negotiation partner; and Israeli polls indicating a dissonance between the people's electoral behavior and their political desires. The argument has been cogently made that Sharon's election in 2001 was made possible, in part, by an apparent or perceived Palestinian rejection of peace with Israel; and that, likewise, persistent popular support for the draconian measures imposed by Sharon was partly a result of Palestinian acts of violence. According to this argument, therefore, a pressure-based "repellant" dynamic was set in motion, in that Palestinians, though the weaker of the two parties, actually contributed negatively through their actions to the formation of the other party's identity—whether by producing a different protagonist altogether (Sharon in place of Barak), or by producing a negative public attitude (for example, support for building the separation wall). It is easy to surmise the effect of such a repellant dynamic on the Israeli negotiating posture, and the negative outcome of such negotiation for the Palestinian side. By the same token, we can surmise the effect of a hypothetical attraction or gravitational-pull dynamic: the more positive changes it might bring about in public attitudes or in negotiations. In short, the protagonists' identities or postures are major variables in a political context or a negotiation or a conflict. Drawing on the way a moral lever functions, we do not take these identities as fixed or rigidly preset, and we assume that enemies or friends are *made,* not *found.* We also assume that a positive negotiating partner is often made, not found—and can indeed be *lost* after having been made or found. (Needless to say, this principle is just as valid in human relationships such as marriage or friendship as it is in political contexts.)

Unless, therefore, one views one's *own* acts as fatalistically predetermined or statically preset and lacks faith in one's ability to make a positive difference, there is clearly a political and psychological space in which one can apply one's will to influence the identity and/or the position of one's opposite in a negotiation or political setting. This is an incredible source of power. But it is a power which can be used in negative as well as positive ways: a protagonist that does not want negotiations to succeed may, through certain actions, so demonize or provoke the other protagonist that the latter can no longer pose as, and indeed no longer even wishes to be, a potential peace partner.

The second element of an Archimedean moral lever is the recognition and positive employment of the distinction between ideology and the more basic layers making up the identities of individual human beings: the distinction between being oneself, in charge of one's meta-biological situatedness, and being a mere example or instantiation of that meta-biological situatedness. For example, opinion polls among both Israelis and Palestinians show overwhelming support for a workable two-state solution. Such support probably reflects the deep-rooted human yearning for peace. But the same polls also show—now probably reflecting another basic human emotion, fear—overwhelming support for those political parties or movements which do not aim at or work toward such a solution. Thus actual political behavior does not correspond with latent dispositions—even when these dispositions are translatable into strong political convictions. Primarily, both Israelis and Palestinians believe the employment of force is necessary, even though they also see eye to eye on what they believe, deep down, is a better solution and a better alternative to continued conflict or the continued use of force. An Archimedean lever in this context, therefore, would, in addition to being nonviolent, employ a gravitational-pull dynamic to draw these latent dispositions to the surface, where they can inform actual, expressed political behavior and attitudes.

Nonviolence as a moral means of effecting political change can therefore consist of both "push" and "pull" dynamics, both pressure and gravitation. But these dynamics must be employed with a view to *transform,* not to *defeat,* the other side. Moreover, in a political system, the use of a gravitational dynamic at the public level can be the best means of generating a pressure dynamic at the leadership level: that is, a public which, in response to a gravitational dynamic, becomes dissatisfied with its leaders' unilateralist policies can apply pressure to change those policies or those leaders in ways that benefit the other protagonist.

The most effective way to employ an Archimedean lever, at least in contexts where a latent positive disposition exists at the public level, is for one party to a conflict, using a gravitational dynamic, to so organize its behavior as to draw out the desired attitudinal change in the other party. This stratagem can, in principle, be employed by either of the two parties. However, given a strategic imbalance between the two parties, or the fact that one party is under the forceful occupation of the other, the option of using this lever is realistically—strange as this may sound—available only to (and in the immediate interest of) the party that is being held down by force. While the "stronger" party risks losing its perceived strategic advantage if it replaces force by a moral lever, the "weaker" party's perceived lack of such an advantage allows it to employ this lever without such risk. But, once the second party sets the moral lever in motion, it becomes in the interest of the first party to embrace this approach as well, and thus to establish a sustainable peace with the other party, as a way to preempt a potential future threat to itself arising from the existing imbalance. Thus although logically the option of embarking on such a conciliatory approach is available to both sides, realistically it is far more amenable to use by the "weaker" side. This leads to an unexpected and rather astounding conclusion: if one defines power as the ability to cause political change to one's own advantage, it is the *Palestinians* who hold this power even though (or precisely because) they are being held down by a mighty military force.

In discussions of ground rules for negotiations between Israelis and Palestinians, the supposed asymmetry in power between the two sides is protested, this always being portrayed as being weighted in favor Israel. But there are more ways than one to view asymmetry, and, in some of these ways at least, the asymmetry which exists may well be weighted in favor of the Palestinians, making us the ones best able to wield the lever that will move our world toward peace.

Epilogue:
What Should We Educate For?

Given my claim in Chapter 1 that it is overly ambitious to hope to trace and understand all the decisions and acts that got us where we are at the moment, it should come as no surprise if I now claim that it is impossible to predict with certainty where we are going. For example, while a two-state solution now seems impossible on practical grounds, it still makes sense to say it is possible in theory, with the gap between theory and practice being any unexpected combination of new decisions and actions, regional or worldwide, that would make what now seems impossible a reality.

"People often forget that politics is not like mathematics," a worldly gentleman told me recently, after I gave a talk sponsored by the Rosa Luxemburg

Foundation in Berlin. "Mathematical problems may have solutions. But in politics, there are only compromises." His observation fits well with the line of thinking I outlined in Chapter 6, namely that reason, by itself, is not a sufficient means for concluding agreements between contending parties. Such points of intersection cannot be predefined mechanistically, and any agreement that takes place will be associated with a unique set of human circumstances which make it happen. Such "agreements" pervade our lives, from the personal, like love and marriage, to the political, like the Egyptian-Israeli agreement reached by Sadat and Begin in 1978. Sadat's dramatic visit to Israel at that time was almost an act of political magic. It couldn't have been foreseen. It was an unexpected leap of faith that succeeded in restoring movement to a political process that had seemed hopelessly deadlocked. Sadat had *faith* that he could change history. And so he did!

One outstanding feature of British public schools is said to be that they build self-confidence in students. At the age of sixteen, when I first attended such a school, I suddenly found myself being addressed by teachers and elders as *Mr.* Nusseibeh or *Sir.* It seemed crazy at first, but over time I realized that this courtesy was part of an overall approach intended to build self-respect and then self-confidence by giving pupils the sense that they were "masters"—*young* masters to begin with, but definitely masters. I am not saying that Palestinian schools should copy all that. But the emphasis on self-confidence is not, as I have discovered in later life, a measly matter. Looking back over my years of watching and getting to know generations of Palestinian university students—in classes and seminars, across tables in smoke-fogged hummus restaurants, in political meetings clandestine and otherwise, and in my own home—I am struck by the change in their general character since the establishment of the Palestinian Authority. Before, students (and political activists more generally) seemed poised and ready to take on the world. Neither Israel's Army of Occupation nor the U.S. government—and not even their own PLO leaders—seemed to them to be insurmountable obstacles in the path they had chosen to take. Plotting and planning in small groups in dorm rooms, café corners, or sparsely furnished student apartments, they believed they could overthrow entire political and institutional edifices. And in a way they succeeded: by fomenting, organizing, and leading their people's uprising against the occupation, they made a major impact on Israel's by then twenty-five-year-old rule. Had it not been for that uprising in 1988, the circumstances would not have existed that today make the search for a two-state solution politically respectable on the world stage. Those young Palestinian students had faith in themselves, faith that they could change history. And so they did. This at a time when no establishment analysts or futurologists, in Israel, the Arab world, or abroad, foresaw the turn of events that "minor" political actors would bring about.

Two decades later, however, that faith seems to have vanished, both among students and in the population at large. The change seems to have begun as soon as the Palestinian Authority was installed and began to construct official Palestinian leadership edifices. Somehow, almost imperceptibly, people began to turn over the power they had possessed and exercised during the uprising to the various arms of the newly established Authority. It may have been a real-life case of the "contract" posited by eighteenth-century political theorists, in which the people supposedly willingly relinquish their sovereignty to a ruler, becoming subjects rather than free and independent actors. Indeed, as I witnessed that transformation in the mid-1990s, I still entertained the naive hope that the Palestinian Authority would, exactly for that reason, feel it owed its le-gitimacy and its very existence to the people, and would therefore be an instrument of the people's will in a way unknown elsewhere in the Arab world. Unfortunately, however, and by some mysterious political chemistry, after ceding their power to the Authority, the people—including, foremost, the young people—forgot that their counterparts in an earlier generation had created that Authority, and that their power, even though they had handed it over, was still latent in themselves and their succes-sors. It was as if the meta-biological being the peo-ple had created had managed to rob the people of their wills.

This brings us back to the importance of self-confidence, and of the faith young people must pos-sess that they are not helpless pawns of larger forces, but are individually and collectively capable of charting their own courses in life, and even of shap-ing history. This faith in themselves may be the most essential tool needed by the next generations of Palestinian youth, and it is therefore the *sine qua non* of what their education should be about.

I realize that education also has other functions to perform. Many of our youth are primarily drawn to what they perceive as prestigious professions, such as medicine, law, and engineering. Educational policy makers, concerned about society's need for technical skills, encourage the establishment and expansion of vocational training centers and technical colleges. And western funding agencies, attentive to reports of human rights deficits and a culture of violence in the Arab world, support special courses on democracy, human rights, and conflict-resolution or negotiation skills. All these facets of education are, to one extent or another, warranted. But, again, I believe that what our students need most is faith in themselves—and faith that they have it within themselves to shape history. No single or magic formula exists for nurturing this kind of faith, but surely it involves learning to respect oneself, and therefore others, first as individual human beings and then also as public actors or creators (very much like what Hannah Arendt describes as being a citizen in the classical sense). Surely it involves learning to respect life and the acts of creation that life brings—in the arts and the sciences, in politics, as well as in private instances of human warmth and sharing.

Palestinian society is largely bottom-heavy, with about a third of its population of 3.5 million attending classes at one level or another. There is no want of subjects to study at schools or first- and second-level degrees to pursue at universities. Much has been made of the need to change or upgrade teaching techniques and skills. And much is being done. But what remains undone, what remains in need of doing, is to remind people of their own strength: to make education the means by which Palestinian youth come to realize they can take their destiny into their own hands. How this is to be done, *that* it is done, and that, in consequence, Palestinian destiny of Palestinian making begins to unfold—all this is work for the next generations.

Notes

1. How Did We Come to This?

1. One of the first discords one encounters in study-
ing the Israeli-Palestinian conflict is one of numbers,
namely of how many Arabs and how many Jews lived
in the region in any given period. The estimate provided here is consistent with most reports, and it is
likely that after the First World War, in response to
the economic and infrastructural development un-
dertaken by the British, the area received migrants
from neighboring Arab countries roughly in proportion to the new Jewish immigration from Europe.

2. Banned from living in Jerusalem during the Byzantine period, Jews may have first been allowed to return to the city by none other than the second Muslim caliph, Caliph Omar himself. In Geniza, upper
Egypt, in 1923, archaeologists excavating the ruins of
a synagogue dating from the Middle Ages found a

declaration by a rabbi hailing Caliph Omar for planning to lift the ban. According to the Greek Orthodox Church records that are usually cited in this context, he did not do so: while promising to uphold the rights, practices, and holy places of Christians, he reaffirmed the ban on Jews. Unfortunately, no copy of the caliph's original document exists in Muslim archives, and historians (including Muslims, beginning with al-Tabari, d. 923 c.e.) rely on the Church's copy. But whatever Caliph Omar's role may have been, it was under Islamic rule that Jews were allowed to return to live in Jerusalem.

3. The designation "Arab," describing an ethnolinguistic population, preceded the designation "Muslim," and although Islam became the religion of most Arabs, being Arab is not inconsistent with belonging to any religion (or to none), including being Christian or Jewish. Indeed, Jews who inhabited the Islamic-Arab world were Arabs in the cultural-linguistic sense, and some of the great Jewish thinkers, such as Maimonides, were as much Arab in that sense as they were Jewish in the religious sense; see Sarah Stroumsa, *Maimonides in His World: Portrait of a Mediterranean Thinker* (Princeton, 2009). Closer to the period we are discussing, the indigenous Jewish presence in the Arab world made itself felt in politics (for example, in the Iraqi Communist Party), business (for example, in Iraq and Egypt), and literature. While the Jewish minority did not enjoy a perfect political existence, yet relations never deteriorated to the inhumane and life-destroying levels reached in

Europe. Indeed, the very concept of anti-Semitism, or "the Jewish problem," arose as a European issue and was arguably exported to the Middle East through British policy (described later in this chapter). For a discussion of Jewish life in the Islamic-Arab world, see Mark Cohen, *Under Crescent and Cross: The Jews in the Middle Ages* (Princeton, 1994).

4. In his controversial book *The Invention of the Jewish People* (Verso, 2009), Shlomo Sand argues that even the famous Exodus probably involved only a limited portion of the Jewish population, the rest continuing to live dispersed throughout the land. More generally, it is likely that the region's population over the centuries has been a mixture of races and ethnicities, with one Abrahamic religion sometimes being adopted instead of another by the same subgroup.

5. Religion as such was not part of the early Zionist program; in fact, Zionism was initially—and in some quarters, continues to be—opposed by some religious Jews for daring to take on God's work: God, not man, was supposed to resurrect Zion and rebuild the Temple.

6. The Ottoman administrative structure consisted of geographic districts called *sanjaks,* each with a central governorship responsible for running local affairs. These governorships were connected to a regional capital, and these in turn to the so-called High Portal in Istanbul. The area that later became Mandatory Palestine comprised three *sanjaks.* One of them, whose governorship was in Jerusalem, was an independent administrative unit directly linked with the

High Portal. It covered the region from the Jerusalem-Jaffa axis in the north to the Sinai in the south. The other two areas were north of that axis: one included parts of present-day Lebanon and had its governorship in coastal Akko; the other included parts of present-day Jordan and had its governorship in Belka. These were run by the High Portal through the regional capital, Beirut.

7. Women have always been active in Palestinian life as political leaders, artists, painters, civil society organizers, and literary figures. One of the first female Arab students in Cambridge (U.K.) in the early twentieth century was Anbara Salam Khalidi (1897–1986), a member by marriage of one of Jerusalem's most prominent Palestinian families. The first-ever translation into Arabic of Homer's *Odyssey* was done by her.

8. Members of this well-trained British regiment later formed the military forces that served the Zionist project—often, as in the 1946 terrorist bombing of the King David Hotel (the British administration's Jerusalem headquarters), at the expense of the British.

9. The provisions of the 1922 Mandate Britain was granted by the League of Nations made explicit Britain's intention to establish a Jewish homeland in Palestine. The Mandate also affirmed the need to protect the civil rights of "existing non-Jewish communities in Palestine." The latter provision, rather than a truncated two-state solution, may still be the best available interim measure of reaching peace, as

will be suggested later in this chapter and in Chapter 6.

10. U.N. General Assembly Resolution 181, November 29, 1947.

11. Shashi Joshi, *The Last Durbar: A Dramatic Presentation of the Division of British India* (Oxford, 2006).

12. See Tamar Hermann, "The Bi-national Idea in Israel/Palestine: Past and Present," *Nations and Nationalism* 11, 3 (2005): 381–401.

13. The Oslo Accords granted the PLO limited rule, first in Gaza and Jericho and then gradually, over a period of five years, in the rest of the territories occupied by Israel. The idea was that after five years the Palestinians would have complete independence.

2. What Makes Life Worth Living?

1. Aziz Abu Sarah, "A Palestinian Remembers the Holocaust," available at *http://www.commongroundnews. org.*

2. Yizhar Be'er, "Human Tragedy as a Catalyst for Change," and Mona Eltahawy, "The Loneliest Man in the World," both available at *http://www.commongroundnews.org.*

3. What Are States For?

1. National Committee for the Heads of the Arab Local Authorities in Israel, *The Future Vision of the Palestinian Arabs in Israel* (2006).

2. These settlers' calculations go far beyond their own

well-being, material or spiritual. For many of them, bringing about the Jewish Kingdom of Israel, and ensuring *its* well-being, is a divine mission which it is their duty to fulfill. Even their vision of the state itself, fully realized, and complete with the rebuilt Temple in place of Islam's Noble Sanctuary, is not the cause to which such zealots devote their lives: that cause is Yahweh and Yahweh's post-state plan for humankind. (This is not to say that all zealot settlers are deeply religious. There are also nonreligious settlers who view the state as existing for *them*, whether as a chosen people or simply as Zionists.)

4. Can Values Bring Us Together?

1. Amin Maalouf, *In the Name of Identity: Violence and the Need to Belong,* translated by Barbara Bray (Arcade Publishing, 2000).

2. Avi Issacharoff, "Hebron Settler Riots Were Out-and-out Pogroms," *Haaretz.com,* December 5, 2008.

3. In trying to compile such a list, we might draw on the scientific work of the Harvard evolutionary biologist Marc Hauser, who has proposed the existence of what he calls a "universal moral grammar." See, for example, Marc D. Hauser, *Moral Minds: How Nature Designed Our Universal Sense of Right and Wrong* (HarperCollins, 2006).

5. What Does the Future Have in Store?

1. One exception was the Communist Party, which, in line with official Soviet policy, supported partition.

In Israel the Party consisted of both Arab and Jewish communists and represented a vocal but marginal political minority. (In Jordan, by contrast, it was outlawed and therefore almost silent. As a self-described international movement, communism was not very popular in the newly "patriotized" Arab world.)

6. Who Runs the World, "Us" or Thugs?

1. John Horgan, "Winning the Ultimate Battle: How Humans Could End War," *New Scientist*, July 7, 2009.

7. How Can We Move the World?

1. See Melanie Kirkpatrick's interview with former U.S. Defense Secretary James Schlesinger in the *Wall Street Journal*, July 11, 2009, in which Schlesinger muses about the possibility of "extending the [U.S.] nuclear umbrella to the Middle East in the event that the Iranians are successful in developing that capacity." Such comments should raise even more concern in this regard.
2. M. K. Gandhi, *Hind Swaraj or Indian Home Rule* (1909), chapter 17.
3. Ibid., chapter 15.

Acknowledgments

This book synthesizes much of what I have learned, both formally and informally, over many years. Apart, therefore, from my most immediate teachers and sources of inspiration —my life companion, Lucy, whose encouragement, gentle guidance, and cogent comments have been, as always, indispensable; my sons, Jamal, Absal, and Buraq; and my daughter, Nuzha—it would be impossible to list all the very special individuals and institutions whose influence on my thinking, and therefore on this book, has been formative.

Even so, I would like to mention my own institution, al-Quds University, and my academic and administrative colleagues there, for having been tolerant of their president's intermittent absences, of mind as well as of body, while this book was being written, rethought, rewritten, and put through its many revisions. In a financially troubled university whose president is often sought out for answers to pressing questions and demands, it is impossible to overstate the value of this particular discretion by my peers.

I should also single out two institutions where I spent restorative sabbaticals: the Woodrow Wilson Center in Washington, D.C., and Harvard University's Radcliffe Institute for Advanced Study. Without the psychological space afforded by these two esteemed institutions—space for reading, listening, and ruminating, and thus for testing my daily political experiences against the reasoned arguments of other scholars—I doubt whether I would have gotten to the point of putting my thoughts down on paper. I thank the administrators at both institutions for their support—especially, at Radcliffe, both Drew Faust and Judith Vichniac. I would also like to thank Paul Rahe, whom I met during my Woodrow Wilson sabbatical, and whose prolific political scholarship and intermittent visits to al-Quds University have been a continuing a source of education for me. And Homi Bhabha, Melissa Franklin, Claire Messud, and Sylvie Delacroix, all of whom provided support and encouragement during my sabbatical at Harvard. Each of these four, in different settings—over delicious meals cooked by Homi and by Melissa, during smoking rounds of the Radcliffe quad with Claire, and in animated discussions about constitution-making on the office steps with Sylvie—has contributed to the evolution of my thinking, and has thus sown in me a seed of eternal gratitude. I particularly thank both Homi and Sylvie for their invaluable comments on earlier drafts of the book.

But the book might well have remained just another pile of papers had it not been for my editor at Harvard University Press, Sharmila Sen, who, with the wily craft of a "thought miner," managed to extract, then to reorder, the thoughts and observations that were buried in that pile of papers.

Sharmila's intellectual compass (if I may change the metaphor) mapped my path from notes to manuscript. Her later choice of Camille Smith as developmental editor couldn't have been more apt, and was immediately vindicated as obtuse ideas magically became comprehensible and convoluted passages became readable. My gratitude to both miner and refiner cannot be overstated. Needless to say, any residual limitation was determined by the content and quality of the mine itself. Here I accept, with due recognition of all possible prior causes, my own share of responsibility.

Index